THE COMPLETE WALKER

Kevin Walker

ASHFORD
Southampton

To Vic and Madeline –
two of the best Walkers!

Published by ASHFORD
1 Church Road, Shedfield, Hampshire SO3 2HW

Whilst great care has been taken in the compilation of this book, neither
author nor publisher can accept responsibility for the use, or
consequences of the use, of the information and opinions expressed
herein; nor for any inaccuracies or mishaps arising from the work.

British Library Cataloguing in Publication Data
Walker, Kevin
    The Complete Walker.
    1.   Recreational: Walking
    I.   Title
    796.5'1

    ISBN 1-85253-123-1

Typeset in 11/12pt Garamond
by Acorn Bookwork, Salisbury, Wilts
Printed in Great Britain

Contents

Illustrations

Introduction

How, you may ask, can anyone write about something as natural as putting one foot in front of the other, that most basic of modes of transport? The notion of such a book may appear even more far fetched when one considers that the experience of walking is essentially an individual one and can be all things to all men: a means of keeping fit; a Sunday afternoon ritual; a way of exploring the countryside; or of 'recharging the batteries' – somewhat paradoxically, perhaps, relaxing via physical exertion.

The Complete Walker is based upon over ten years' professional experience of all forms of walking, from simple strolls lasting little more than an afternoon, to strenuous, high-level mountain treks taking two or three days. I have tried to distill the walking experience into what I consider to be its component parts. Although I have neither the right nor the ability to tell you how, when, or where to walk, what I have tried to do is give you information which may help to make the walking experience more comfortable, satisfying and enjoyable. In this way both those new to walking who are looking for guidance in planning walks, and those who seek to develop their knowledge and skills of the activity will hopefully find something of interest in the following chapters.

For the purposes of clarity and ease of reference, I have divided this book into six sections. The first describes the walking experience, looking at each aspect in detail and discussing what is involved in terms of experience, clothing and equipment. Although several of the divisions might seem somewhat arbitrary, definite distinctions can be made. Not only is each particular type of walking described in terms of the pleasures to be gained, but suggestions are also made regarding suitable footwear and cloth-

1

ing, advice given on the types of equipment available, and mention made of any specific techniques or special skills which may be useful.

Part II describes the wide variety of footwear and clothing available, looking in detail at the different types of walking boots and shoes, and discussing the principles of the layer system of insulation. Part III is concerned with the various items of equipment which may or may not be required, depending upon the type of walk being undertaken, the prevailing weather conditions and so on. In each case it is important to understand what this equipment does, how it works and why it is needed.

Although walking is, in many ways, a perfectly natural activity, there are a number of basic techniques and special skills which you may find useful in certain situations. These are discussed in Part IV. One of the most important skills is using a map and compass. I hope to demonstrate that reading and interpreting a map and using a compass is not only easy, but also fun, and is one of the fastest and surest ways to increase the enjoyment and satisfaction which you can gain from each walk.

The fifth section looks at safety factors. Walking accidents are relatively rare, and it is widely accepted that when they do occur they are usually caused by ignorance of the dangers rather than by stupidity or a lack of common sense. Part V is concerned not only with the recognition and avoidance of a variety of potentially fatal medical conditions, but also with a number of minor annoyances and discomforts, some of which can become more serious if not treated or alleviated at an early stage. Last but by no means least, there are four appendices comprising the Countryside Code, the Mountain Code, a list of useful organisations together with their addresses, plus several suggestions for further reading.

I do not pretend to know everything there is about walking, and the contents of this volume are, of necessity, based largely upon my own experiences and my, perhaps peculiar, personal preferences. However, if having read or browsed through this book, you feel that there are any glaring omissions or inconsistencies, if you find any mistakes, or if you have any comments, critical or otherwise, I would be only too pleased to hear from you.

PART I

The Walking Experience

1

Out and About

I am lucky enough to live in the heart of the countryside. Within two minutes of leaving my front door I can wander along quiet country lanes surrounded by green fields and sparse woodland; a further ten minutes and I can reach open moorland leading onwards and upwards towards a high, windswept plateau, dotted with boulders and sheep, where it is possible to stroll for hours on end without seeing any sign of habitation, let alone another walker. However, you do not have to live in the country to enjoy walking. Wherever you are based the important thing is to get out and about. If you have no car, think of using public transport or walk within walking distance of your home. And when you are walking, don't just use your legs; use your eyes and ears as well.

Many people gain their first (or perhaps only) experience of walking by strolling along quiet country roads. Despite the omnipresent motor car, such walking has several attractions and is likely to awaken a curiosity about aspects of the human (industrial archaeological) and natural (flora and fauna; geology) landscape through which you are passing. One of the easiest ways to begin this highly pleasurable process of self-education is by making use of certain types of waymarked trails.

Waymarked trails

Although any signposted footpath can be described as a waymarked trail (the most obvious example being the long-distance footpaths such as the Pennine Way or Offa's Dyke Path) in this chapter we are more concerned with the variety of very much shorter, often more 'formal' excursions which are offered by nature trails, industrial heritage trails and suchlike. Typically, these trails follow well surfaced paths, along which there are indic‹ posts at points of special interest. They are usually (but ¡ always) circular, many have parking and other facilities at or n‹ the start, and there is often an informative guidebook or leafl available to help the visitor make the most of the visit. Waymark‹ trails fall broadly into two distinct categories: **nature trails** an‹ **heritage trails**.

Taking heritage trails first, wherever I walk, be it in the mountains or lowlands, I am continually astounded by the past works of man, and by the ways in which he has left his mark upon the environment. The isolated, long-ruined croft in a remote corner of the Scottish Highlands; the unexpected lead mine in the fastnesses of the Cambrian Mountains; the slowly silting hammer-pond hidden in a thicket in the Surrey Weald. To me, such exploration and wonder is just as much a part of the walking experience as looking at the 'natural' features of a landscape.

Although it is perhaps somewhat invidious to single out any one particular such trail (there being so many of great quality through-

1. Waymarking is usually of an excellent standard on the National Trails

out the country), the Vivian Quarry Trail in the Padarn Country Park, at Llanberis in Snowdonia, is an excellent example of a heritage trail. Apart from the fact that there is an atmosphere so tangible that it is almost bound to engender an interest in the industrial archaeology of the area, the views on every side have an impressive, wild and open quality that is usually associated only with the most rugged of routes.

Like heritage trails, nature trails tend to vary quite considerably in quality. Many of the best lie in specially designated areas such as national nature reserves, although there are plenty of great quality which have been both designed and waymarked by devoted volunteers from local conservation groups. As with the heritage trails, it is unfair to single out any one site, but the nature trail at the Old Winchester Hill Nature Reserve in Hampshire is one of my favourites. Situated in a delightful area of chalk downland, this trail offers relatively easy walking with extensive views of the surrounding countryside, and the features of interest are well described in an excellent and very informative leaflet which is available on site. Heritage interest, too, is here, in the shape of an Iron Age hill fort, and a display board at the entrance explains many of the archaeological features that can be seen.

Another type of waymarked trail worth mentioning is forest trails. With increasing acreages of Britain's forests being opened up to the public for recreation, there is a greater selection of waymarked trails being offered. These usually start from a convenient point such as a car park and picnic area. As with other forms of waymarked trail, the quality of both the waymarking and the route itself can vary considerably, with routes changing according to the economic operation of the forestry business.

Although there are many excellent forest trails, some with indicator posts and accompanying leaflets, many are simply waymarked routes taking you along forest roads from where you can enjoy the scenery. Trails in forests situated on the steep sides of deep valleys are often more scenic than those which hug flattish areas or valley floors where there are fewer panoramic views and the possibility of feeling 'hemmed in' by trees.

Clothing and equipment

For both walks along country lanes and waymarked trails there is little need for special clothing. A pair of Wellington boots might be found useful if the weather is, or has recently been, wet. (Fairly deeply cleated soles are an advantage in slippery, muddy or especially steep conditions.)

2. *A young party enjoying the spectacular scenery of the Brecon Beacons National Park*

You might consider buying a small, lightweight daysack for carrying waterproofs, warm clothing, light snacks and, perhaps, a flask of drink. However, try to resist the temptation to fill your rucksack to capacity simply because there is room! By the time you have weighed it down with bird and flower identification books, maps, binoculars, a camera, and other 'indispensables', you will find it becomes a nagging weight and starts to spoil your enjoyment. One of the keys to enjoyable walking is to carry only the bare essentials.

Finally, once you start walking along tracks and paths rather than roads, it will be useful if you try to think of the length of walk in terms of time taken rather than distance. For the same distance, it will take you longer to get back to your starting point (or destination) when you are walking along a rough track where there may be gates or stiles to negotiate than if you simply have to walk down a surfaced lane. If you make a habit of keeping track of time regularly and noting your progress on your map, on occasions when the weather takes an unexpected turn for the worse, you will be in a better position to decide whether to hot-foot it back to the car or to look for some form of shelter in the immediate locality.

Following footpaths

The British footpath network is the most concentrated in the world, consisting of almost 200,000 km of footpaths and bridleways along which the general public has a legal right to walk. Despite the protection supposedly given to them by law, however, many public rights of way are impassable, having become overgrown or even deliberately obstructed. It is only by using the footpaths that the network can be maintained for future walkers.

Local walking guidebooks or leaflets, although to an extent selective or subjective, can be useful as a confidence booster in route planning, or, when visiting a place for the first time, to get the feel for an area fairly quickly. A good guidebook should significantly increase your enjoyment of an area, saving you time and effort by doing the basic research for you; the better books will give you useful facts and figures about public transport and accommodation, places to visit and things to do, as well as interesting information about things seen during the various walks it describes.

Having followed all the routes described in your guidebook, you may feel the desire to strike out for yourself and devise your own circular trips using the footpaths which you already know. This will inevitably lead you to follow less well trodden ones, at which point some skill in planning and preparation, map reading, map interpretation, and various other navigational skills will be appropriate (see Chapters 11 and 12).

Maps are useful both for making sure you are on course and to check that you are, in fact, following a public right of way and therefore have a right to be walking where you are. Additionally, by consulting your map fairly regularly, you will be able to note local features of interest which you might otherwise have missed. Generally speaking, the Ordnance Survey Landranger maps (at a scale of 1:50,000) will be more than adequate. However, if you require more detail, you should consider using the larger-scale Pathfinder maps (1:25,000). Further details of maps, map scales, and the use of compasses will be found in Chapter 12.

Once you depart from the beaten track with any sort of regularity, you will become familiar with the obstacles to the walker:

paths in a terrible state of repair with, for example, long sections of deep mud; stiles which have all but collapsed or, worse still, foot bridges which are so rotten they are dangerous. The path you have chosen to follow may be so little used that it has all but disappeared into a tangle of undergrowth. Indeed, some paths have become so neglected and overgrown that they have literally disappeared altogether, leaving little if any sign of their original route other than a line on a map.

In these types of situation, it will be helpful if you know a little about your rights as a walker, and about the law regarding public rights of way.

The walker and the law

Generally speaking, the only paths along which you have a legal right to walk are the public rights of way. If you look at the legend on any Ordnance Survey Landranger (1:50,000) or Pathfinder (1:25,000) map, you will find that these are shown differently to other paths and tracks; indeed, just because a path or track (or even a road) is shown on your map, it does not mean that you have any right to follow it. However, in some areas negotiations between one of any number of organisations or local authorities and the landowner have resulted in 'Permitted' routes along which the public may walk. Some of these permitted paths are seasonal, that is to say that the public only has access to them at certain times of the year. The 'closed seasons' are commonly at such times as lambing, or during the rough-shooting period. Any such restrictions should be mentioned in local guidebooks, and there may well be signs at either end of such paths, or at major junctions.

Although the Ordnance Survey maps make excellent guides to the presence (or otherwise) of legal rights of way, they are not legal documents in themselves and have been known to be wrong (mainly because of the impossibility of producing maps that are totally up to date; see Chapter 11). If you wish to check that a path is, in fact, a right of way, you must consult the definitive maps which are kept at County Council and District Council offices, and at some major libraries. These will show any changes that have taken place since the Ordnance Survey map was printed.

The most obvious form of a public right of way is the **public footpath**, along which anyone may walk without hindrance. You can take a pet with you (within reason), but you are not allowed to ride a horse or a bicycle. Next comes the **bridleway**, along which the public may walk, lead or ride a horse, or ride a bicycle.

If you are walking along a bridleway and meet a person on horseback, remember that they have just as much right to be there as you. Similar considerations apply to people riding bicycles. One problem facing the walker is that intensive use of a bridleway by horses and, to a lesser extent, by cyclists may result in a surface which bears an uncomfortably close resemblance to a mud-bath. Indeed, on one bridleway near my home used very intensively by pony-trekkers during the summer months, I have seen wet-weather walkers disappear up to their knees in a foul mixture of mud and horse manure! Motorists and motor cyclists should note that it is illegal to drive or ride on footpaths or bridleways without the express permission of the landowner, and that without such permission all forms of motorised vehicles are confined to within 15 yards of the public highway.

A further right of way is that of the byway open to all traffic. More commonly known as '**green lanes**', these may offer delight-fully simple walking unless they are frequented by the local four-wheel-drive club, in which case they will almost certainly be noisy, smelly and muddy. They may even be dangerous while there is a perfectly legal cross-country 'rally' taking place, espe-cially if the surface is at all muddy or slippery. Although walkers, horse-riders, trials riders and motorists all have a legal right to proceed in their own way along such routes, it is often difficult to reconcile the different modes of transport.

The final category (apart from the public highway) is the '**RUPP**' – the Road Used as a Public Path. There are so many rules and regulations governing these that many are now being redefined as either footpaths, bridleways or byways. Generally speaking, these, too, are open to all traffic (although this is not always the case), and there is invariably no problem with regard to access for pedestrians.

Who is responsible?

The County Council has a legal obligation to signpost each foot-path where it leaves a metalled road, although few councils appear to have undertaken this task with anything like the required amount of enthusiasm. Indeed, the surface of the path 'belongs' to the Highway Authority (and hence the County Council), and maintenance of this surface is the County Council's responsibility, although the local parish or community councils may also be involved. Gates and stiles are the responsibility of the landowner, and grant aid is available to help him keep them in good order. If he neglects to do the necessary work, the County Council is empowered to do it for him and to charge him the full cost.

A landowner cannot close or obstruct a path in any way, unless this is due to ploughing. In this case, he must inform the County Council of his intentions at least seven days in advance, and make good the surface of the path afterwards. Unfortunately, few landowners bother either to give notice or to reinstate the path, and fewer councils take any notice anyway.

If you are a bona-fide walker and you find that the path you are following has been blocked, you are legally entitled to remove enough of the obstruction to allow you to pass. If this proves impossible, you should find a convenient way of bypassing the obstruction. Either way, you should report any obstructions to the Highway Authority or County Council, the Ramblers' Association, and – where relevant – the National Park authority or similar local body. If you are keen on litigation, you can bring a private prosecution alleging obstruction!

There are two specific cases worth noting. Firstly, when a path has been obstructed or obscured by crops, many people will be tempted to walk around the edges of the field in order to do as little damage as possible. Unfortunately, although a thoughtful thing to do, if you leave the route of the right of way the landowner can sue you for trespass. You are, however, perfectly within your rights if you walk in single file through the crop, following the line of the right of way, and doing as little damage as is necessary to allow you to proceed.

Secondly, the law regarding bulls is not as simple as many people think. Indeed, it can vary quite considerably from area to area. Although most counties have bylaws which prohibit the pasturing of most breeds of bull in fields crossed by public rights of way, certain breeds are exempt, and it is often the case that bulls are allowed in such fields so long as there are cows present as well! The logic in such cases is that the bull will be so interested by the cows he will not concern himself with mere mortals. However, having been chased by an overgrown and aggressive lump of beefsteak in just such a situation, I am always very wary of bulls, no matter how amorous they may seem initially.

If you are chased, do not try to be a hero. One useful nugget of information is that bulls have difficulty in stopping or turning on a down slope, so try to use the contours to your advantage, and get out of the field as quickly as possible. If you are hurt, especially if the bull is pastured illegally, you should inform the police.

Clothing and equipment

On moderately demanding terrain you do not really need expensive or specialised walking gear. However, as mentioned above, some paths, particularly the more popular bridleways, can be quagmires, and walking shoes can be a distinct disadvantage in such conditions. I have seen well-shod people walk through such patches and emerge on the other side in stockinged feet, their walking shoes having been devoured by the mud! If you are walking for any distance or with any regularity you might like to consider buying a pair of lightweight walking boots, or even a more sturdy variety (see Chapter 4), which have the advantage of being somewhat more water-resistant than their lightweight counterparts.

Obviously, you will need a map and, possibly, a compass, together with any notes which you may have made. A waterproof and spare sweater will be necessary and, if you are going any distance, a little food and drink. You might also like to consider taking a small first-aid kit (see Chapter 14) – very useful on paths which have become overgrown with brambles!

Whilst on the subject of overgrown paths, you may well find a pair of waterproof overtrousers worth their weight in gold if you follow the less frequented paths in late spring. Particularly during or shortly after wet weather, forcing your way along heavily overgrown paths can be like wading through a lake – the vegetation around you holds so much moisture that, without overtrousers, you will soon be saturated. If the vegetation is high, or the path leads between hedges, you may well find that you have to wear your waterproof jacket as well!

2

Long-distance Walking

Many people consider long-distance footpaths to be a challenge, whether purely one of completing the distance or of finishing in the shortest possible time. However, there is nothing particularly special about long-distance footpaths; although many have an overall identity in that they follow (sometimes approximately) a natural or historical feature of some description, each path is little more than a long line of public rights of way which have been linked together and given a common name like 'The Pennine Way' or 'Offa's Dyke Path'. Only a few individuals walk along such paths with the intention of completing the entire length in one go; the vast majority of walkers cover only a short section at a time, using the path like any other. As it happens, this fact is often used as a major argument against the development of long-distance footpaths and National Trails. Opponents argue that, because of the attendant publicity, long-distance footpaths tend to get used far more than the rest of the network, and this results in a situation which is bad not only for the long-distance footpaths (which get heavily used and therefore badly eroded), but also for the remainder of the footpath network (which gets relatively little use and therefore decays through neglect). It is undoubtedly the exhalted status which long-distance footpaths wrongly enjoy which has caused so many of their problems, not least those of erosion – an increasingly serious problem on all the popular paths. I personally feel that those who view long-distance walking as a form of time trial, should ask themselves whether they would not gain just as much enjoyment by covering the same distance around a convenient running track or park – thereby reducing footpath erosion.

Official and unofficial long-distance paths

There are essentially two types of long-distance footpath: 'official' paths (as approved by the Secretary of State for the Environment), and a growing number of 'unofficial' long-distance footpaths (developed either formally or informally by local authorities, individuals or local groups). At the time of writing, the Countryside Commission has proposed to expand the number of official long-distance footpaths in England and Wales, and rename them 'National Trails'. It is also proposing that the look of the public rights of way network as a whole be dramatically altered by developing local paths, parish paths, local networks and regional routes – this latter category quite possibly to include (and therefore arguably give a certain amount of protection to) some of the better unofficial long-distance footpaths. Although these proposals (put forward by the Countryside Commission in a consultation paper) have caused a fair degree of argument, there is little doubt in my mind that, in the long term, such argument and discussion can only be of benefit to both the footpath network and the walking community as a whole.

There are currently (1989) thirteen 'official' long-distance footpaths in England and Wales (see Figure 3). The oldest and perhaps most well known of these is the **Pennine Way**. Running from Edale to Kirk Yetholm, a distance of just over 400 km it is a high-level route passing through three national parks, and is still regarded by most people as the path which offers the greatest challenge. It is not an easy route: the terrain is often rugged, more akin to mountain walking than strolling along a footpath, and people contemplating walking long distances on this path in particular should be aware of the demands which will be made on them, especially during bad weather.

Offa's Dyke Path follows the approximate line of the often impressive eighth-century earthwork which mirrors (more or less) the present boundary between England and Wales. Running from Chepstow to Prestatyn, it is the variety of scenery throughout its 270 km which gives this path much of its attraction. However, like the Pennine Way, it often passes through rugged and mountainous terrain and a number of sections are demanding and should be approached with respect.

The **Cleveland Way** runs from Helmsley to Filey, a distance of 150 km. The route is divided into two distinct sections: the Coast Path, following one of the most dramatic and rugged parts of the

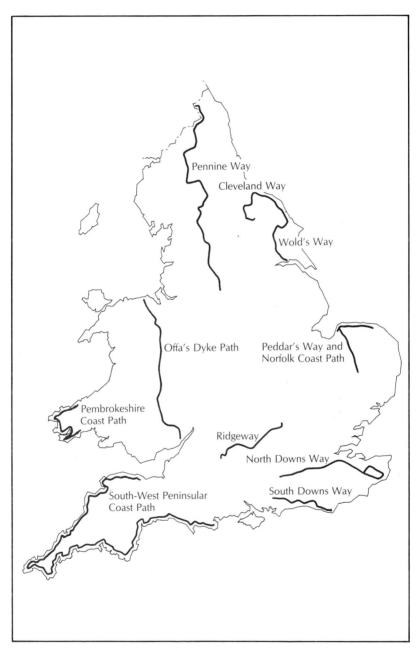

3. *National Trails in England and Wales (1989)*

east coast, and the somewhat more demanding Moors Path, which travels through the delightful Cleveland Hills. This latter path should be approached carefully during bad weather conditions. The **Wolds Way** can be usefully regarded as a continuation of the Cleveland Way. Running from Filey to Hessle and the Humber estuary, a distance of just under 130 km, it travels through the delightful Yorkshire Wolds, giving pleasant and comfortable walking throughout its entire length.

The **Pembrokeshire Coast Path** was the third long-distance footpath to be opened. Just under 300 km in length, it stretches from Amroth to Cardigan and takes the walker through what can only be described as some of the most impressive coastal scenery in Europe. Unfortunately, not all of the coastline is accessible to the public due to the presence of the armed forces, and access is restricted along one of the finest sections when NATO forces have fun and games practising blowing eastern bloc tanks to pieces. Apart from needing to get your timing right here, you also need to bear in mind the tides and work to a schedule. The wrong state of tide can mean a long wait or a lengthy detour inland!

The **South-West Peninsular Coast Path** is really a combination of five separate long-distance footpaths: the **Dorset Coast Path** (116 km from Sandbanks to Lyme Regis); the **South Devon Coast Path** (150 km from Lyme Regis to Plymouth); the **South Cornwall Coast Path** (214 km from Plymouth to Penzance); the **North Cornwall Coast Path** (217 km from Penzance to Marsland Mouth); and the **Somerset and North Devon Coast Path** (132 km from Marsland Mouth to Minehead). There is a breathtaking range of scenery of all descriptions to be seen throughout the total distance of over 800 km, but its length inevitably means that this path in particular is rarely completed in one go. Indeed, the heaviest use tends to be by holidaymakers following relatively short sections, although it undoubtedly makes a stupendous expedition if you have either the time or the inclination.

The **Ridgeway** stretches for just under 140 km from Overton Hill to Ivinghoe, following the line of one of the most important of the ancient routeways. Unfortunately, some of its length is classified as a by-road, and what was once pleasant, tranquil walking is increasingly being spoiled by hoards of roaring Range Rovers, screaming Suzukis and manic Mitsubishis! Although I freely admit that they have as much right to be there as the walkers, I find the arrogance and selfishness which is displayed by a minority of these drivers utterly incomprehensible.

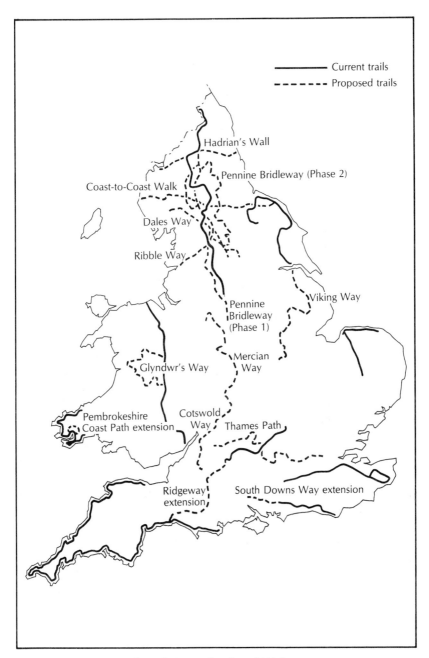

4. *Proposed National Trails in England and Wales*

The **North Downs Way**, at present the closest long-distance footpath to London, is another ridgeway of great antiquity, its route including the Pilgrim's Way to Canterbury. Running from Farnham to Dover, a distance of almost 230 km, the route offers gentle walking with superb views over the Weald and the 'garden of England'.

The **South Downs Way** is unique amongst the present long-distance footpaths in that it is also a bridleway for its entire length. Traversing the warm, green and impressively rolling countryside between Eastbourne and Buriton, it offers 129 km of pleasant and largely gentle walking through often spectacular chalk downland.

The **Peddars Way** and **Norfolk Coast Path** stretches in two sections between Thetford and Cromer, the sections meeting at Hunstanton, and the total distance being some 150 km. The inland path follows Peddars Way, an ancient Roman road, whilst the coast path traverses Norfolk's northern coastal areas, complete with salt marshes and waders.

The Countryside Commission's planned series of National Trails includes up to fourteen additional routes (see Figure 4). Although the final outcome depends on both finance and the approval of the Secretary of State for the Environment, the Countryside Commission is committed to four of these trails, these being the Thames Path, an extension to the South Downs Way, a Pennine Bridleway, and a trail following Hadrian's Wall.

The Thames Path will stretch for over 250 km, following the line of the River Thames from its source in Gloucestershire into the very heart of London. The 40 km extension to the South Downs Way will take it as far as Winchester, thus making it a far more attractive and accessible trail. The footpath following Hadrian's Wall will stretch for approximately 120 km from Newcastle-upon-Tyne to the Solway Firth, through a landscape of exceptional historical and scenic interest.

Of interest to horse-riders and cyclists as well as walkers, the Pennine Bridleway would be developed in two stages, the first being on the Countryside Commission's 'list of priorities'. Although the exact route is still to be defined, Phase One will be approximately 400 km in length and will stretch from Ashbourne to Henshaw. Phase Two would add a series of loops to the northern part of the bridleway, giving a number of alternative journeys.

The remaining proposals form a shortlist from which new trails would be selected. They include two extentions to current official long-distance footpaths: one to the Ridgeway (160 km to link the present route with the South-West Peninsular Coast Path at Lyme Regis); the other to the Pembrokeshire Coast Path (a further 100 km around the mysterious yet beautiful Daugleddau Estuary). Many of the proposals are based on routes already popular with walkers, some of them being well established unofficial long-distance footpaths such as the 300 km **Coast-to-Coast Walk** across northern England. This stretches from Robin Hood's Bay to St Bees and follows the line of Wainwright's popular walk. The **Dales Way**, of approximately 130 km, is another good example. Already shown as a long-distance footpath (LDP) on Ordnance Survey maps, and offering excellent accommodation facilities along its length, the path runs between Ilkley and Bowness on Windermere in the Lake District, with linking paths from Leeds and Bradford.

Further examples of popular routes now likely to get official recognition are the Cotswold Way (covering some 160 km of 'green and pleasant land' from Chipping Campden to Bath), and the Mercian Way, which would run for over 200 km from the northern end of the Cotswold Way to Mow Cop in Cheshire, following the existing Heart of England and Staffordshire Ways. The Ribble Way, an existing recreational route of 70 km along the River Ribble from Gisburne to Preston, also falls into this category.

Recognition, too, is to be given to Glyndwr's Way, a 200 km path which loops westwards from Knighton and Welshpool on the central section of Offa's Dyke Path as far as Machynlleth, passing through spectacular mountain scenery which is rich in legend and folklore.

The Viking Way, on the other side of the country, is the final route on the shortlist. Currently an unofficial path approximately 230 km long, this travels through much of the Lincolnshire Wolds, linking with the Wolds Way at the Humber Bridge, and with Hereward's Way – another unofficial long-distance footpath – at its southern end. If you take into consideration that Hereward's Way links with the Peddars Way, and the Wolds Way links with the Cleveland Way, you will begin to appreciate the scale of the walking network which the Countryside Commission seem keen to promote.

The situation in Scotland is somewhat different, with laws on access to the countryside and rights of way in general making any form of long-distance footpath a highly controversial subject. The only official long-distance footpaths which are fully open at the present time are the 150 km **West Highland Way** which runs between Milngavie (on the outskirts of Glasgow) and Fort William, and the **Southern Uplands Way**, a coast-to-coast walk of some 340 km which runs from Portpatrick to Cocksburnpath. As one would imagine, both these paths have sections which are fairly strenuous.

Two other proposals have been made: the Speyside Way, planned to travel the 96 km between Spey Bay and Glenmore, is still not fully open despite being officially designated in 1978. Although access negotiations are still continuing, only the first 48 km between Spey Bay and Ballindalloch are open to the public. The other proposal is for a Great Glen Way which would run between Fort William and Inverness, a distance of just over 100 km. All these paths have been rigorously opposed by many of the more traditional hill-goers from both north and south of the border. Details of the current position of the long-distance footpath network can be obtained via the addresses given in Appendix III. Whatever the arguments for and against, there can be little doubt that long-distance footpaths and National Trails are here to stay – the trunk roads and motorways of the footpath network.

Using long-distance footpaths

Although official and unofficial long-distance footpaths have much in common, there can also be major differences between the two types of path. Official footpaths will usually be documented by at least one official guidebook, with waymarking done by means of the Countryside Commission's 'acorn' symbol. Signposting is generally of a high standard and the path is reasonably well maintained. Unofficial paths, on the other hand, do not always have an accompanying guidebook and the standard of waymarking can vary dramatically. On occasions it may be ambiguous or even non-existent. Furthermore, stiles, gates and footbridges may be in an appalling state of disrepair, with the path itself overgrown or ill defined, leading to access problems, and any accompanying guide may be of little help, being both inaccurate and unclear.

Fortunately, such situations are increasingly rare. Where paths have been designed and developed by the more formal bodies such as rambling clubs and local authorities, signposting is generally very good, especially where the Countryside Commission's colour scheme has been adopted. This marks footpaths with yellow arrows, bridleways with blue arrows, and byways with red arrows. The more formal routes may also be waymarked with some form of symbol, which can be almost anything from a picture of a walking man to a design of local significance. The Dyfi Valley Way, for example, is waymarked with doves, whereas the Cotswold Way is waymarked with white circles.

There are places, however, where such waymarking becomes inappropriate, this being particularly true where the path leads you into high mountain areas or across open moorland. In such areas it is more usual for the route to be delineated by the occasional pile of stones or 'cairn'. Unfortunately, and particularly in popular areas where a number of different paths may cross in otherwise featureless terrain, cairns may be evident in profusion. Such overzealousness has led not only to the immediate surroundings losing much of their once wild attraction, but also to a meaningless proliferation of confusing piles of stones. Indeed, in certain areas, and especially in conditions of poor visibility, following cairns may do little more than encourage you to walk in ever-decreasing circles! An alternative system of spray-painted symbols on rocks is, of course, nothing short of vandalism.

The 1986 edition of the *Long Distance Walker's Handbook* lists some 231 unofficial long-distance footpaths in England and Wales alone – which indicates the rapidly growing popularity of leisure walking. However, as already mentioned, most people walk only relatively short sections of such paths. Assuming a basic level of fitness, most people will find that they can comfortably walk at least 20 km in one day. The average time taken to complete the Pennine Way, for example, is therefore nineteen days. Since it is always advisable to leave a few days spare in case of exceptionally inclement weather or the unexpected, three clear weeks would therefore seem to be the minimum period needed for this particular route – a sizeable chunk of most people's annual holiday. On the other hand, half the official long-distance footpaths can be completed during a period of one week. Of the others, the South-West Peninsular Coast Path, for example, can be broken down into its five sections, and it is possible to complete the remainder by breaking them down into more manageable lengths. Additionally, many of the unofficial routes can be completed in a week or indeed a long weekend.

Planning the walk

With all walking, but particularly when walking long distance, it is important to realise that 20 km on the map does not necessarily mean 20 km on the ground. Map distance does not take into consideration all the ups and downs of hill and vale, and this can make a surprisingly noticeable and often unwelcome difference to the distance you actually walk. This is especially true of coastal walking, where headlands and inlets may increase the length of your walk to more than twice the apparent map distance. Planning an extended route can therefore be quite an awesome, although satisfying, task. Initially, you may prefer to walk with part of a group or by means of events such as The Ultimate Challenge, an organised and unique 'do-it-yourself' walk from coast to coast across Scotland. In this event the route is between two given points, one on the west coast, the other on the east, the choice of route between the points being entirely up to the individual. Some people choose to walk at a high level whereas others prefer to stick to the valleys and glens. The main advantage of this event is that there are other people around you doing similar things, and that excellent back-up is available in case of problems or emergencies. (The vast majority of 'challenge' walks have more in common with orienteering than with rambling, being purely speed trials in which you are required to complete a given route within a set time or to pass a number of checkpoints, again within a given time.)

Once you have gained a modicum of experience on the better paths, you may discover the urge to strike out by yourself and plan your own route. Although your basic reference source will be Ordnance Survey maps (initially at a scale of 1:50,000; subsequently perhaps, the larger-scale 1:25,000 maps), you will also need to consult a variety of guidebooks, footpath leaflets and so on, and you may well find it useful to write for further information to local authorities, tourist information centres, or the secretaries of local rambling clubs.

One of the major considerations is that of managing pace, especially when walking distances of more than about 10 km. Many people, particularly enthusiastic youngsters and those who have had little experience of walking, set off from the start at a pace which they cannot hope to maintain all day, eventually getting slower and slower as time runs on and energy runs out; far better to maintain a steady, rhythmic stride throughout the walk. Obviously, the techniques you will need will depend upon the terrain through which you pass: in quiet country lanes and wide tracks simple plodding will suffice; where the path is ill defined – on open moorland or between the outcrops and crags of a rocky mountain ridge – you will find it useful to have practised the various techniques described in Chapter 10. As will be seen later, your situation can rapidly become extremely serious if you are caught unprepared by bad weather and poor visibility in open moorland or high mountain areas, and this is true no matter how well defined your path. A good working knowledge of navigation skills (see Chapters 11 and 12) is therefore essential.

3

Trackless Walks

Heathlands and Moorlands

One of the major attractions of trackless or open countryside is the overwhelming sense of freedom and remoteness found there. Particularly in the higher moorland areas such as Dartmoor, South Wales and parts of the Pennines, there are often few landmarks to give any sense of scale, and, with certain important exceptions, the works of man are noticeable mainly by their absence. The lack of fields means that there are few boundaries to hem in the walker apart from stone walls which seem so ancient and solid that they have become as much a part of the landscape as the rocks and boulders from which they were made.

Lowland heaths offer excellent practice grounds in which to sharpen up your map interpretation and compass technique – essential skills if you plan to go mountain walking or to visit the larger, higher or more remote moorland areas. By this I mean you should have the ability to navigate accurately across all terrains and in all weather conditions by means of a map and compass, and be skilled enough to find a 3 m diameter pool in the middle of a vast and otherwise featureless expanse of moorland.

The difference in the demand made on the walker by the lowland heaths and upland moors is never more apparent than during bad weather or when visibility is poor. For example, because moorland scenery is relatively featureless, accurate navigation requires a fair degree of skill, even in good visibility. Finding adequate shelter if you are caught unexpectedly by a storm can also be difficult; some moorlands are so vast that it will not be easy to retreat if the weather does change unexpectedly.

Thinking of distance in terms of minutes rather than miles becomes doubly important when forsaking the beaten track and striking off across country. On Dartmoor, for example, it is easy to get into a position where one is a good 10 km from the nearest habitation, and although when following roads or the better-defined paths such distances can be covered in about two hours, it is difficult to make such speedy progress across the moors. Any bad weather inevitably slows down the walker: the wind may be against you, making your every footstep an effort; in all probability you will be tired, and you may even be unsure of your exact position. In such situations, not only may you become exhausted, but there is also the risk of hypothermia, particulary if you are poorly equipped or tired, or cannot find adequate shelter. (See Chapter 14.)

Perhaps the biggest difference between walking across the moors and walking along paths or tracks is the amount of energy needed. The nature of moorland terrain, where there may be thick heather to grab at your ankles or tussocks to throw you off balance, means that each step requires just that little bit more effort. Over several kilometres this can make a surprising difference. In addition, keeping your balance over uneven ground may mean using seldom-worked muscles, which can lead to all sorts of problems if you are not reasonably fit.

Clothing and equipment

When walking in areas where you are likely to find yourself several miles from the nearest habitation, and where conditions underfoot are difficult, choice of footwear, clothing and equipment is obviously important. In my view, some form of walking boot is essential, since walking shoes, however sturdy, not only fail to give sufficient support to the ankles, but may also give inadequate protection to the rest of the foot. An additional factor is that sand, heather and pieces of grit working their way down the sides of shoes is somewhat annoying, if not downright painful! (See Chapter 4 for a full discussion.)

If footwear is important, so too is clothing. Here again, if you are simply spending a Sunday afternoon strolling around a lowland heath, your basic walking kit of spare sweater and waterproofs may suffice. On the other hand, if you are off across Dartmoor or visiting a similar high moorland area elsewhere, it will be sensible to take a few extra items, particularly a windproof jacket of some description, and although the final choice of clothing is largely personal, applying the 'layer system' is a useful approach (see Chapter 5).

With regard to equipment, as already discussed, you should avoid weighing yourself down with unnecessary items. Assuming you are out for the day, your basic kit will consist of the items described so far: map and compass, some food and a flask of drink, any personal items which you may wish to take along and a small first-aid kit. For more remote areas, a polythene survival bag, whistle and some emergency food should also be carried (see Chapter 7).

Mountain walking

For me mountain walking is set apart from other forms of walking by the sense of achievement and deep satisfaction I gain through it. The ever-changing aspect of mountains makes each journey a new joy. But mountain walking is far more than simply looking at views: it also has to do with the joys of exploration and adventure, with the warmth of camaraderie, with personal challenges and achievements, and – for some – with the uncertainties of risk and danger. It will demand more from you than almost any other type of walking. Consequently, a good level of fitness is required, together with some knowledge of walking 'techniques' (see Chapter 10) and detailed planning and preparation. Needless to say, a book is no substitute for experience and, as already mentioned, I would recommend developing the various skills and techniques in relatively gentle terrain before setting out on the more ambitious journeys.

Solo walking in mountain areas entails a degree of risk, not because you are more likely to have an accident when walking by yourself (indeed, many experienced solo walkers believe that they are less likely to have an accident because they take more care), but because if an accident does occur the implications are more serious and you will be left to your own devices. For instance, if you were to stumble and twist your ankle (something that can happen to anyone, no matter how experienced), it could take several very long and painful hours before any help reached you. Weather conditions could easily be such that you run the risk of hypothermia. Indeed, such conditions should be regarded as the norm.

It is therefore preferable if you can undertake your first few trips with more experienced companions, or with one of the many clubs which cater for novices. Alternatively, and especially if you prefer walking in a small group, you might consider going on a

5. Mountain ridge walking — one of the most spectacular types of mountain walking

course to learn about 'mountaincraft', or to gain experience of specific techniques such as mountain navigation or security on steep ground. (See Appendix III.)

Clothing and equipment

Clothing, footwear and equipment should be chosen with the worst weather conditions in mind. Good-quality walking boots, with at least one pair of thick woollen socks or stockings, should be regarded as essential for all but the most simple ascents on gentle, rounded summits using well defined paths.

Clothing should consist of several insulating layers (including one spare layer) covered by some form of windproof shell (see Chapter 5). You will also need a full set of waterproofs (including waterproof overtrousers), a woollen hat and mittens. Although there is no reason to prevent you wearing shorts and a running vest on those rare, hot summer days, you should always carry spare clothing with you, for mountain weather conditions can change with remarkable suddenness.

With regard to equipment, weight is still your enemy, and you should avoid encumbering yourself with unnecessary items. In addition to those items which you would normally carry in your rucksack (i.e. spare clothing and waterproofs, map and compass, food and drink), you would be well advised to carry a simple first-aid kit and whistle, survival bag and some emergency food. (See Chapter 7 for a full discussion of these.)

Mountain safety is basically a matter of common sense, and the vast majority of people will come to little harm. The following guidelines may be useful, however:

1   Get local advice about the terrain and about the walk you intend to do.

2   Leave word of where you have gone and when you intend to be back (and never forget to let people know when you are back).

3   Get a local and up-to-date weather forecast and be prepared to stay in the valleys if the forecast is bad.

4   Never be afraid to turn back if you think the situation demands it. The thought 'it will be a shame to turn back now because we must be nearly at the top' has been responsible for countless accidents and a number of deaths, as has the 'it will never happen to me' syndrome.

Until you have had some experience and know what to expect from various situations, the best advice I can give is to say that if you are unhappy or unsure about doing something, don't do it!

Backpacking

To many people, particularly those who enjoy long-distance walking, backpacking is what it is all about. The most simple definition of backpacking would be 'living out of a rucksack'. The assumption here is that the backpacker will be camping, and will therefore carry everything necessary for the journey in a rucksack, including a tent, sleeping bag and sleepmat; stove and various items of cooking equipment; sufficient food and drink either for the entire journey or to last between places where fresh supplies can be bought, and a whole host of other odds and ends. Although there can be little doubt that many people consider the camping experience to be one of the great joys of backpacking, others find the thought of sleeping under canvas totally alien, in which case a

6. *The backpacking rucksack. Note the way in which the rucksack hugs the body and mimics the contours of the spine, thus allowing the walker to carry quite heavy loads*

form of long-distance backpacking without a tent may be appropriate.

Backpacking without a tent

One way of organising a backpacking walk that does not rely on camping is to use some of the slowly but surely increasing number of camping barns and bunk-houses. In this case you will still need to carry your sleeping bag and food, and perhaps even some cooking equipment. A rather more sophisticated alternative could be to stay in bed-and-breakfast accommodation (often in local farms, some of which offer exceptional value for money) or even in luxury hotels! In between these two extremes are youth hostels where there is often a good level of comfort (albeit shared), and which usually offer a choice between ready prepared meals or self-catering.

In all cases it is advisable to check on accommodation availability before setting off. When following the more popular routes at the height of the season, it may also be advisable to book accommodation in advance. There is nothing quite so frustrating as wandering tentless around an unknown village at half-past eleven on a wet Saturday night having discovered that all possible forms of local accommodation are full. Sleeping under a dripping hedge after a day of looking forward to a hot bath and clean sheets is guaranteed to put the dampers on the best of walks!

Finding out about local accommodation in all but the most popular of areas can sometimes be a problem. If you find this to be the case, your best sources of information will be your map (which marks youth hostels, and some of the more remote hotels and inns), local guidebooks, the handbooks of motoring organisations and suchlike, tourist information centres and the local parish or community council.

Backpacking with a tent

Legally, you are not allowed to camp anywhere in Great Britain without the permission of the landowner. Here again, your map can help, for it will usually show some (but not all) 'official' campsites. Failing this, try to find a guidebook or write to the local council. Alternatively, it is often possible to find a suitable site on arrival. There can be little doubt that this gives a tremendous sense of freedom, for you do not have to reach a particular place by a particular time, but can wander along at will. Knocking on the local farmhouse door is often highly successful, and the vast majority of farmers are often only too happy to let you pitch your tent in a corner of one of their fields – as long as you ask first. Indeed, on several occasions, having done just this, I have been woken in the morning by stupendous and extremely welcome gifts of a hot breakfast and a large pot of tea!

Long-distance backpacking is not an ideal way to gain an introduction to camping. If, as is distinctly possible, a lack of routine or experience leads to the novice's gear getting wet on the first night, the remainder of the trip may degenerate into a soggy and very uncomfortable experience. For this reason you might consider early journeys in the company of someone with greater experience of the activity.

Although discomfort is something which, in itself, is not too serious, if it is your sleeping bag or spare clothing which gets wet, the situation is potentially dangerous. This is especially true on backpacking trips where camps are sited on high ground or in remote areas. In such circumstances, unless you have a warm sleeping bag and some dry clothing into which you can change at the end of each day, there will be a risk of hypothermia.

PART II

Footwear and Clothing

4

Choosing Footwear

Boots or shoes?

There is no one solution when it comes to footwear. From the point of view of general walking, boots are not always essential and if your walking consists solely of travelling relatively short distances along country lanes, well laid paths, and low-level or urban trails, then a good pair of walking shoes or sturdy trainers will usually be ample. If, on the other hand, you intend to leave the well beaten track and follow the rougher paths, or even to strike out across trackless terrain, you would be well advised to give your feet and ankles the extra protection provided by a walking boot.

So how should you decide whether you need boots or whether shoes will be adequate? The easiest way is to ask yourself a number of questions about the type of walking you intend to do. *What will conditions be like underfoot?* If you are always going to be walking along roads, not only may boots be unnecessary, but you may also discover that sturdy shoes or well designed trainers are better. *What is the likelihood that you will tread awkwardly*, leading to the risk of a turned ankle (or worse)? Obviously, all things being equal, you are less likely to damage your ankle when walking along a road or a well laid path than when struggling across a boulder field or tussocky moorland. One advantage of boots over shoes is that they do tend to give more support to the ankles. Boots should therefore be the natural choice if you intend to cross rough terrain. *Do you plan to walk regularly*, no matter what the weather? Trainers and puddles are not the ideal combination, and shoes and mud can be even worse. Although there is little to prevent you wearing Wellingtons when going for short walks during wet weather, they are not the most comfortable of things to have on your feet during the longer trips, and you may well find that boots are better. *How far will you be travelling?* If you regularly walk more than about 6 or 7 km you will find that your footwear needs to be of a fairly good quality, whatever its type. If you walk wearing anything less, not only do you run the risk of it falling apart on you during your walk, but, in the long term, you are also far more likely to suffer from discomfort, or even from some form of injury to your feet or ankles.

There are any number of other questions which you can ask. Ultimately, the final decision can only be made by you, and should be based upon the premise that the rougher the conditions underfoot, the more important it becomes for you to wear boots.

If you decide that you need boots, you will still have a choice to make. As you will see if you visit any specialist outdoor shop, there is an impressive range of boots on the market, some designed to do one particular job, others designed for more general purpose use. Modern methods of boot construction are currently changing the face of outdoor footwear; however, I think it is safe to predict

7. *The range of walking boots available can be bewildering*

that for some time to come there will be three separate types of walking boots available, these being lightweight boots, boots of a more traditional construction, and plastic boots.

If, on the other hand, you decide that your walking is of a type which does not require you to wear boots, you will have to choose between a pair of sturdy shoes (which may or may not have been designed specifically for walking), or a pair of good-quality trainers. Each are described in more detail below.

The right fit

For both shoes and boots, ask to see a range of models and discuss the pros and cons of each. (Do not forget, however, that most specialist shops will carry a far larger range of boots than of shoes.) When you come to try on the footwear, the most important consideration is that you should be comfortable. For most people this means wearing one or more pairs of thick woollen socks. Make sure you take your socks along with you. Alternatively, many outdoor shops have 'trying-on' socks available for customers' use. Start with a pair of shoes the same size as your normal shoes, choosing a larger or smaller size afterwards if necessary. Once you think you have found the right fit, take a walk round the shop and see how your feet feel. If they do not feel comfortable after ten minutes or so, they are certainly not going to feel right after several hours' walking.

In addition to the general comfort, there are certain things of which you should be aware. *Does your heel move?* If so, the fit is slightly too large and may well give you heel blisters. *Do your toes feel at all cramped?* If so, the fit is too narrow, and not only do you run the risk of blisters across the tops and sides of your toes, but walking may become excruciatingly painful after only a few miles. *Can you feel the end of the footwear with your toes?* If so, the fit is too small, and not only will you find that walking downhill is extremely painful, but you also run the risk of losing your toenails. In addition to the above, there are several factors which are peculiar to certain types of footwear, and these will be discussed in the relevant sections.

Aftercare

Once you have bought your footwear, you will obviously want it to last as long as possible. After each walk, check the condition of the laces, replacing them if necessary, remove any grit and mud which may have become trapped in the sole, and clean the uppers.

Suede is best cleaned with a stiff brush, leather with a damp cloth. Allow the footwear to dry slowly in a cool, airy place, well away from any sources of heat. On no account try to speed up the drying process by leaving wet footwear in drying rooms or on radiators, for the leather will become hard, even brittle, and may crack. When dry, leather uppers should be given a coat of a good-quality wax polish or a proprietary boot proofing compound, paying particular attention to any seams. Avoid using liquid proofings over prolonged periods for these will over-soften the leather. You may also find it helpful to use a specialist conditioning compound every few months. With regard to suede and fabric uppers, there is very little that needs doing apart from an occasional (ozone-friendly) spray with a silicone proofing compound.

Walking shoes and trainers

For trainers and walking shoes, sports shops are usually a better bet than the average high-street shoe shop. However, you may find that while you can get expert advice on trainers suitable for road running and jogging, the staff are not so knowledgeable when it comes to the requirements of the walker. Additionally, although most sports shops carry a far wider range of trainers than the average specialist outdoor shops, only a few carry a good range of walking shoes. My advice, then, is to visit a specialist outdoor shop, whenever this is possible, as they are usually run by enthusiasts who know what they are talking about and who will not only be able to show you a range of suitable models, but will point out the pros and cons of each. The choice between trainer and shoe will then be much easier.

In choosing a pair of trainers I would advise you to avoid those constructed largely of plastic. Apart from the fact that plastic uppers tend to make your feet sweat (and may therefore lead to an increased likelihood of blisters, athlete's foot, smelly feet, and various other nasties), if used on a regular basis it will not be many miles before the trainers start suffering from plastic fatigue and start to split. Far better and, in the long term, more cost effective, are those trainers in which the uppers are made predominantly of suede, possibly in conjunction with small panels of fabric woven from either man-made or natural fibres. Although such trainers will not be 100 per cent waterproof, many are water-resistant to a quite remarkable degree.

For walking shoes, uppers made from leather are far superior to those constructed from man-made materials, for similar reasons to those described above. Additionally, it is worth noting that a shoe with few seams is better than one with many because, no matter how well proofed it is, a seam represents a weak spot both in terms of the strength of the shoe and its ability to keep out water. This being said, many excellent walking shoes are designed in such a way that the sides and top are made from separate pieces of leather. If you choose a model of this type, you would be well advised to pay particular attention to this top seam when you are cleaning and reproofing.

Regardless of whether you choose shoes or trainers, there are a number of further aspects which should be taken into consideration:

(i) *Type and thickness of the sole.* This should protect the base of the foot from sharp stones, pebbles and other objects which may be trodden upon, but – perhaps less obviously – it must also provide a cushioning effect each time the foot touches the ground. This is particularly important if you walk predominantly along roads. Good trainers are often far better in this respect than similarly priced walking shoes, and although it is possible to buy walking shoes with specially designed air-cushion soles, these do tend to be expensive. If you have decided in favour of a walking shoe but cannot justify the price of one with a cushion sole, shock-absorbing insoles are available, which, although expensive, usually work out cheaper than if you had bought a special cushion-soled shoe.

(ii) *Stiffness of the sole* will play an important part in the comfort of your footwear, especially during longer walks (see Chapter 4). It is worth noting here that both shoes and trainers should be stiff enough *along* the foot to give a fairly high degree of spring as you walk, and that most of the bending that does occur should take place in the region of the toe joints. In order to give the required amount of support, the soles should also be fairly rigid *across* the foot. If, for example, you hold both ends of the shoes and twist, you should feel considerable resistance. If your shoes or trainers are not stiff enough, you will flop along the road as if wearing a pair of slippers – very comfortable to begin with, but incredibly fatiguing after only a short distance. If, on the other hand, they are too stiff, you will plod along flat-footedly, feeling as if you have planks of wood strapped to your feet.

(iii) *The grip* provided by the sole is an important factor also.

Although, obviously, this is less crucial when walking along roads than in climbing mountains, it can still have an effect both on the enjoyment of the walk, and on the amount of leg-work needed, particularly when the ground is wet or muddy, or when the surface is composed of loose, rounded particles such as those found along recently resurfaced roads and paths. In this respect, deeply cleated rubber soles are generally regarded as being far superior to those of plastic or PVC, and leather soles – still to be found on some shoes – should be avoided at all costs.

Lightweight boots

There can be little doubt that lightweight boots represent the ideal footwear for the vast majority of walkers. They are generally extremely comfortable from the moment you first wear them, rarely needing more than a short period to become 'broken in'. Indeed, some people will tell you that they need no breaking in at all. (I believe this to be incorrect unless, of course, you are lucky enough to find a pair which perfectly matches the contours of your feet from the outset.)

It is possible to distinguish between two types of lightweight boot, each suitable for various types of walking: firstly, models in which the uppers have been constructed from suede and fabric, and secondly, those in which the uppers are made entirely of leather.

(i) *Suede-fabric lightweights* are suitable for all occasions where you would usually wear shoes, and can also be used on the less well trodden paths and easier (low-level) long-distance footpaths. It should be noted, however, that none are waterproof to any noticeable degree, and although some manufacturers have tried to get around this problem by using a waterproof (or breathable) material for the fabric panels, I have yet to come across any model in which this has proved successful over any length of time. A further limitation is that many of these boots give surprisingly little ankle support and only a modicum of protection for the foot, and are therefore far from ideal for use in rocky or tussocky terrain. If you decide to buy a suede/fabric lightweight, you would therefore be wise to check such factors very carefully.

In terms of durability, I would recommend the most expensive model you can afford, for there are some diabolically constructed apologies for boots at the cheaper end of the market. Whilst some of these boots may seem attractive, it is of little use buying a

8. Lightweight walking boots. This is the most modern design, in which the cut-away heel has been replaced with a more traditional block heel

9. Traditional-style walking boots

10. Plastic boots. Although successful for serious winter mountaineering, the type of plastic boot currently available is not really suitable for more general walking

'bargain' if the fabric panels tear or the seams start to split after the first 20 km or so.

(ii) The better *leather lightweights* are superb boots which are suitable for walking in virtually all types of terrain during summer conditions, although you should take note of the limitations mentioned in the final paragraphs of this chapter. The best of these boots will be expensive, and although cheaper versions are available, the quality both of the construction and of the leather can vary considerably. It is very much a case of paying your money and taking your choice.

As with leather walking shoes, the more seams there are, the weaker and potentially less waterproof the boot. The very best models use a single piece of leather for the main body of the upper. The problem with these 'one-piece uppers' is that larger pieces of leather are proportionally more expensive than smaller ones, and some manufacturers have therefore designed models which are cut low around the ankle, thus reducing the area of the one-piece and (supposedly) keeping down the cost. Unfortunately, such designs greatly reduce the amount of support available to the ankle, although the better models do incorporate a fairly substantial ankle cuff which does much to alleviate the problem.

For all lightweight boots, there are a number of features which will be found useful:

(a) A *'sewn-in' or 'bellows' tongue* (which will help to prevent the ingress of water) is virtually essential in the British climate, and, for similar reasons, the laces should not pass through the boot via eyelets. The most convenient method of lacing makes use of two forms of attachment: *'D-rings'* keep the laces in position on the forward part of the boot, whilst *'speed-hooks'* enable you to get into and out of the boot without too much difficulty.

(b) The *stiffness of the sole* is at least as important for boots as for walking shoes (see relevant paragraphs in both the previous chapter and the next). Although such stiffness is very much a matter of personal preference, it is safe to say that the rougher the terrain you intend to cross, the stiffer and more substantial should be the sole. The most rigid lightweight boots have leather uppers and will probably lie towards the top end of the price range.

(c) A further factor which is worth bearing in mind when choosing such boots is whether or not you will need the option of resoling. For cheaper models, especially where moulded soles are used, resoling is difficult if not impossible.

Almost without exception, lightweight boots are fitted with

'monobloc' soles (see Figure 8). These were hailed by many as the new wonder sole when they first appeared, and some manufacturers claimed that they would reduce footpath erosion yet still maintain the same frictional qualities as the more traditional soles. Recent evidence would appear to suggest that some of these claims were slightly exaggerated. From personal experience I have no hesitation in recommending lightweight boots for general walking in summer conditions, but have found that the grip given by monobloc soles can be inferior to more traditional designs, particularly on steep, grassy ground during wet weather. There is no doubt in my mind that lightweight boots are totally unsuitable for winter use on anything more difficult than well trodden valley paths.

Traditional boots

We have already noted that although lightweight boots are ideal for many walking conditions, they have a number of limitations, particularly with ankle support and grip. As conditions underfoot become even more extreme, particularly with regard to roughness and steepness, so grows the need for footwear which is more robust, supportive, and possibly stiffer than the average lightweight boot, and offering 'a fraction more traction'. This need is best met by a boot constructed along more traditional lines.

Traditional boots invariably have leather uppers, and the sole, which should be of the 'Vibram' or 'Commando' type (see Figure 9) is attached to the body of the boot via a mid-sole. The precise form of the construction varies from model to model, but is usually done either by a form of welding, by screws, stitches or adhesive, or by a combination of two or more of these methods. This method differs from lightweight boots, where the sole is in the form of a 'footbed' which is almost always bonded to the main body of the boot with some form of adhesive. Consequently, traditional boots are almost always heavier and more robust than their lightweight counterparts. (An exception is to be found in the cheaper, imported boots of traditional design which make use of moulded, plastic soles and which cannot be successfully resoled.)

The stiffness of traditional boots can vary from totally floppy to totally rigid. In the not-so-distant past, this stiffness was regulated by a 'shank', and boots were sold either as half shank, three-quarter shank, or full shank. Nowadays, modern plastic compounds are being used with increasing regularity, and although this has decreased the amount of breaking-in required by these boots, traditional models usually require far more breaking-in than lightweight models with soles of a similar stiffness.

One of the questions asked by people choosing a good pair of boots for the first time is how firm or flexible should they be. There are no hard and fast rules about this.

Although, generally speaking, the rougher the terrain, the stiffer should be the sole, there comes a time when increasing the rigidity of the boot becomes counter-productive, and the stiffest boots are usually only suitable for winter mountaineering use. The reason walking boots need a certain amount of flex should be fairly obvious if you watch someone walking barefoot. Assuming that the person is not flat-footed, you will notice that the front third of the foot bends, allowing the person to spring forward from the toes.

Do not be seduced by manufacturers' advertisements: your first pair of walking boots need not be expensive. For (relatively) impartial advice, a specialist outdoor activities shop run by enthusiasts who have personal experience of the most up-to-date models is the best place to begin. Good-quality walking boots should contain all the features mentioned in the last chapter: the leather from which the upper is formed should ideally be in one piece, there should be a bellows tongue, and the lacing is best done via D-rings and speed hooks. The welt (i.e. the amount of sole which protrudes from around the base of the boot (absent in lightweight boots which make use of footbeds) should be narrow.

One further point worth noting is that if you intend to visit mountain areas during winter conditions, you will need a traditional boot which is robust enough to stand up to the punishment of step kicking, and stiff enough to take crampons. (Such techniques are extremely specialised and are beyond the scope of this book.)

Finally, it is important that you realise that the perfect boot does not exist. For example, what is good for walking across a sandy heath in balmy weather is not going to be suitable for scrambling over snow-covered mountains or trudging across a wet, peaty moor. If you become enthusiastic about your walking, especially if you intend to visit a variety of areas throughout the year, you may like to consider buying two pairs of boots – a lightweight pair for use in lowland and moorland areas during summer, and a slightly more robust, traditional pair for the more rugged terrain and for general use during wet weather and winter conditions.

Plastic boots

Over the past few years, a number of plastic boots have appeared on the market, some of which purport to have been designed for walking. The advantages of using plastic as a material for the upper part of the boot are many, the two most obvious being that such boots can be made completely waterproof, and that they require next to nothing in the way of maintenance.

The most successful of these boots are totally rigid and bear a close resemblance to ski boots, a typical model being shown in the photograph. Containing all the features one would expect from a traditional boot made from high-quality leather, there is little doubt that this type of plastic boot has revolutionised winter mountaineering. In essence, these models consist of two boots in one: a flat-soled, flexible inner boot made from leather, and rigid outer boot, usually with a Vibram sole, made from plastic. Extremely robust, such double boots are lighter, warmer, and far more convenient than their leather counterparts, and have become the standard winter mountaineering footwear within a remarkably short space of time. Indeed, I have no hesitation in recommending them for this use.

At the time of writing, however, I know of no plastic boot which I can recommend for general walking. Although various models have appeared on the market over the past few years, they have all been subject to what can best be described as plastic fatigue! The problem is that, as we have seen, a walking boot needs to be designed in such a way that it allows for the natural spring of the foot, and this necessitates a boot which has some degree of inbuilt flexibility. Leather is an ideal material for the uppers of such boots because it can cope with the constant movement. Unfortunately, the plastics used to date have not been anywhere near so successful, and have tended to split within a relatively short period of time – at which point you might just as well throw away the boot.

Various designs of 'hinge' and 'bellows' have been tried, all without much success, which is unfortunate, because there is little doubt in my mind that a successful plastic walking boot would revolutionise walking footwear to the same extent that the rigid plastic double boots have revolutionised winter mountaineering footwear. Hopefully, a successful design will appear at some point in the future.

5

What to Wear

Clothing should be light and compact enough to fit easily into a rucksack when not being used, yet robust enough to stand the wear and tear which even the simplest of walking entails. When choosing outdoor clothing do not be unduly swayed by current fashion. The important thing, of course, is for your clothing to be functional, keeping you warm and dry whatever the weather throws at you. Obviously, such clothing becomes increasingly important the further you walk. However, your outdoor clothing need not be expensive. Indeed, you probably already have a number of suitable garments hanging in your wardrobe. What is important is that you understand the purpose of these garments.

The human body can be viewed as a machine which needs certain operating conditions if it is to all work efficiently. If the main part of the body or 'core' (see Chapter 14) gets either too hot or too cold, the efficiency of the rest will be impaired. The main purpose of clothing, therefore, is to protect the body from undue heat loss or gain. In the British climate it is primarily protection from heat loss with which we are concerned, and this is best done by using the layer system of clothing.

The layer system is based upon the fact that air is an extremely good insulator. When we wear one garment, it is the layer of air trapped next to the skin, together with air trapped within the fibres of the garment, which keeps us warm. Two garments will trap two layers of air which means, obviously, that two thin garments will be warmer than one thick garment. Apart from the improvement in heat conservation of the layer system a further advantage of building up insulation in this way is that it is easy to adjust the amount of insulation. Until walkers gain some experience, they often find that they are commonly too hot or too cold,

43

and it is generally not realised how important it is to try and maintain a comfortable temperature. Feeling cold means that the body is losing heat; if this heat loss is maintained over any length of time, it can lead to serious problems. Apart from the fact that the body will be using a fair amount of energy in an attempt to redress the balance (with the consequent feeling of fatigue), the inevitable end-product of unchecked heat loss is hypothermia (see Chapter 14).

If, on the other hand, you feel too hot, your body will start sweating in order to try and reduce the heat, and this will cause your insulating layers to become wet, leading to a marked reduction in their efficiency. Although this will cool you down fairly rapidly – which will seem welcome at the time – this reduction in thermal efficiency may also result in a rapid heat loss at a later and perhaps more inappropriate time.

By using the layer system, there should be no excuse for you to feel either too hot or too cold under normal circumstances. It is simply a matter of reducing or increasing the number of layers you are wearing, and anticipating when this should be done. For example, the greater the muscular effort, the more heat you will create, so you will often find it useful to remove a layer before ascending a steep slope. Conversely, you will be producing far less heat when you stop to admire a view, so you should put on an extra layer in order to compensate for this.

Insulation layers by themselves are not enough, however. Saturated clothing, in which water has replaced the trapped air, can transmit heat away from the body at a rate of 250 times that of dry clothing, and this can lead to a phenomenal rate of heat loss. When combined with even a mild wind, the water in the surface layers evaporates, a process which increases the heat loss still further, and the lack of a windproof in these situations can lead to heat being drained from the body at a rate which is potentially lethal. It is therefore necessary to carry a further outer shell made from a waterproof material.

The body also loses heat from the extremities, and particularly from the head which can radiate up to 50 per cent of the body's heat production in certain conditions. In order to be at all efficient, therefore, the layer system must include some form of protection for the head, hands and feet.

Now we have discussed the principles of the layer system, it will be helpful to look at each of the layers in more detail.

Underwear

If you only walk along the highways and byways, you may never need to wear thermal underwear. If, however, you intend to walk in the mountains and moorlands, it is important that you understand the relevance of underwear to your comfort and, in certain conditions, even to your safety. The rapid rate with which wet clothing can transmit heat away from the body is mainly due to the process of conduction, in which heat is transferred between one body and another, combined with the evaporation of moisture in the surface layers. Convection, or the general cooling effect produced when cool air (the wind) passes over a warm object (your body), will also play a part.

Although the wearing of an efficient waterproof shell (see Chapter 5) should protect you from the vast majority of atmospheric moisture, there are two other ways in which your clothing can get wet. Firstly, your body constantly produces moisture in the form of perspiration. Under normal circumstances, this moisture passes through the clothing and evaporates with little noticeable effect, but if you wear a non-breathable, totally waterproof shell, this evaporation will not be able to take place, and the moisture will condense and begin to soak into your insulating layers. Secondly, even if you are not wearing a waterproof shell, if you begin to overheat due to strenuous exercise, the rate at which you perspire may be greater than the rate at which the perspiration can evaporate, and there will be a consequent build-up of moisture in the clothing. In both these situations there is obviously potential for increased heat loss due to wet clothing, and the best way to reduce this potential is by maintaining a dry layer next to the skin, thus reducing the amount of conduction which can take place. The first layer of clothing (i.e. your underwear) is therefore very important.

The best man-made material for this innermost layer is polypropylene, and the fabric from which the better quality thermal underwear is made will be composed entirely of this material. One of the main advantages of using polypropylene is that it allows the passage of moisture from the skin, thereby leaving a dry layer next to the body. The main disadvantage is that clothing made from this material needs fairly careful washing to prevent shrinkage.

The best natural material, wool, has both the advantages of polypropylene (it wicks away moisture from the skin), and disadvantages (it needs careful washing). Such garments can also be unbearably itchy against the skin.

String or cellular vests of one description or another undoubtedly trap a layer of air next to the skin, but they also have the disadvantage that they can be extremely uncomfortable across the shoulders if you are walking with a rucksack for any length of time. Indeed, the heavier the rucksack, the more uncomfortable they become.

Upper garments

Most people will find that the combination of a good-quality shirt or sweat-shirt plus two or more thin sweaters provides plenty enough warmth for the vast majority of situations. It is only when you begin to visit the more remote areas or go for long walks in particularly cold winter conditions that you will need to think about special insulating garments. However, it will be helpful to look at the types of clothing worn in these slightly more extreme situations for, in the long term, there can be little doubt that a well-made garment designed specifically for use in the outdoor environment is going to be superior to something designed for wearing in the high street.

Of all the natural materials available, wool is undoubtedly the best insulator because it retains much of its insulating properties even when wet. Additionally, and somewhat surprisingly, if wool garments do get wet they can actually give out heat due to a complex chemical reaction. The disadvantages of wool are that it can absorb water at an alarming rate, thereby dramatically increasing its weight and needing a long time to dry out. It is also relatively heavy and bulky even when dry; washing can be difficult and pure wool is becoming increasingly expensive.

If you do wear woollen garments, you will find that wearing a woollen sweater underneath a shirt or sweat shirt is far warmer than wearing it the other way around. This is because the close weave of the material traps a large amount of air within the fibres of the wool.

Down or feather garments, either in the form of body-warmers or jackets, have an important role to play in certain specialist situations. However, although weight for weight, they are far warmer than wool, they suffer from the disadvantage that they lose almost all their insulating properties if they get wet. Additionally, the majority of people carrying duvet jackets, for example, use them only as an additional outer layer when they are resting, finding them far too hot to use when on the move. The range of modern synthetic fabrics continues to expand at a bewildering rate. If you are looking for a garment in purple, pink or turquoise, possibly with day-glo stripes and fluorescent zig-zags, look no further! Colours aside, many of these synthetic fabrics are excellent for outdoor use. Nylon fibre-pile, spun synthetic filaments, and fabrics made from polyester and acrylic fleeces are particularly good, and are all (weight for weight) warmer than wool. Like wool, they also retain much of their insulation quality when wet, but unlike wool, they tend to absorb very little water, this being particularly true of polyester and acrylic fabrics. This means that they do not become vastly heavier when wet, nor do they take ages to dry out afterwards. Washing, too, is generally easier than with wool, as long as manufacturers' instructions are followed.

When choosing a synthetic garment you should bear in mind that, generally speaking, garments made from fibre-pile are less wind resistant than those made from fleece materials, and that some of the thinner fleece materials are more wind resistant than the majority of the thick fleeces. With the amount of choice available it can get very confusing. Your best bet is to visit an outdoor equipment shop and tell the retailer what type of walking you do. Ask to see a range of suitable garments, and get him to explain the differences in terms of insulation when wet and dry, wind resistance, durability, ease of washing etc. You should also compare weight and bulk.

When choosing a combination of garments with which to build up the layers, it is important that you think about the ease of ventilation. One popular mix is to use one or more pull-over type garments (possibly with a short zip at the neck) in combination with an outer garment which has a full-length zip. If this type of combination is chosen, ventilation becomes extremely easy, and it will be far more convenient to undo a couple of zips when overheating on a hard, uphill climb than to stop and remove a layer, thereby breaking one's rhythm.

Remember, also, to take the bulk of other layers into consideration when choosing such a garment. A fibre-pile jacket which is comfortable when you are only wearing a tee-shirt will not necessarily be comfortable when you are wearing a combination of thermal vest, woollen shirt and fleece pull-over. In any event, with the possible exception of your thermal underwear (which should be a close fit), all your garments should be reasonably roomy, and should fit in such a way that there is no bunching under the arms or tightness across the shoulders. Although such things will affect your comfort even during a Sunday afternoon stroll round the local park, they become of greater relevance if you intend to visit mountain areas in winter conditions, where any restriction of circulation can be instrumental in causing cold injuries such as frost-nip and frostbite. (See Chapter 14.)

Lower garments

When clothing the lower part of the body you should apply exactly the same principles as when clothing the upper part although, generally speaking, you will not require quite so many layers. One of the main reasons for this is that, whatever the type of walking, you will be working the muscles of your legs fairly hard and will therefore be creating a fair amount of heat through this muscular activity. However, it should, by now, be fairly obvious that excessive heat loss is to be avoided even from this area on all but the warmest of days.

For general walking, tracksuit bottoms (or similar) are ideal. They are light in weight, reasonably warm and cause little restriction of movement. This latter factor, in particular, is important in terms of comfort. To illustrate the point, imagine climbing over a stile wearing a pair of stretchy, tracksuit bottoms; now imagine doing the same thing in a new pair of close-fitting, denim jeans. Even the thought is enough to bring tears to the eyes.

Although thin tracksuit bottoms will be fine for summer use, you would be wise to choose something a little more substantial for use during the winter months, although you can always put on an extra layer (see below).

If you intend to travel slightly further afield, it might be wiser to choose something made from a material which is not only fairly warm, but also reasonably wind resistant. Many people like to wear a pair of loose-fitting trousers made from some form of traditional material, and woollen fabrics such as moleskin and tweed are still fairly popular. However, as we saw in an earlier chapter, woollen fabrics are fairly bulky, become very heavy when wet, and take ages to dry out. Additionally, when used in walking trousers, they can rub and cause painfully sore areas at the back of the knees and along the inside of the thighs.

Modern fabrics are growing in popularity, and there are a

number of excellent polycotton walking trousers available. Although these are extremely light, windproof and quick drying, the unlined models have minimal insulation properties and cannot be recommended for winter use or for mountain walking. However, there are versions available which are lined with a thin fleece material, and these give a surprising amount of warmth for their weight.

Also popular are some of the modern stretchable synthetic fabrics, many of which are also warm and windproof, light and fast drying. Although it is possible to buy walking trousers made from these materials, walking breeches and salopettes tend to be the norm. Breeches are very popular amongst mountain walkers because they cause little restriction of movement to the legs. Worn in conjunction with long woollen socks (or stockings), they also offer the possibility of 'air conditioning' to the legs, for on hot days (or during hard, uphill slogs) the stockings can be rolled down and the bottoms of the breeches left undone.

One problem with wearing separate upper and lower garments is that they can become untucked, and this leads to a potentially cold and uncomfortable area around the waist. Although this problem can be overcome to a greater or lesser extent by wearing extra-long vests or shirts with long tails, etc., salopettes – rompersuits for adults – are the ideal answer. They are extremely comfortable (if rather expensive) and can be bought with either standard length or breeches-style legs.

If you walk in very cold conditions you may well need an extra layer, this usually taking the form of thermal underwear (i.e. 'longjohns') made from either polypropylene or wool. Surprisingly enough, a standard pair of women's tights are only slightly less effective. Also available are trousers made from fibre-pile and from fleece, and these are extremely effective, especially when worn as an under-layer. If worn alone, you should note the earlier comments about wind resistance.

Windproofs

You can spend literally hundreds of pounds on your insulating layers, but it will all be for nothing if you do not have an effective windproof layer to go over the top and keep in the heat. In Britain days of total calm are so rare as to be almost non-existent, and any breeze will cause some of the warmed air trapped between your insulating layers to be replaced by cold air. The stronger the wind, the more air will be replaced and the greater will be the resulting heat loss, and although this can be reduced to a significant extent by wearing several layers made from wind-resistant materials, a good windproof garment should be regarded as an essential item of clothing for all but the most sheltered of lowland walks.

If you are working to a tight budget, there is no reason why you should not use your waterproof shell garments as windproofs, for waterproof materials are invariably windproof, although this does not necessarily work the other way around. However, there is a problem when using your waterproofs in this way, because an effective waterproof garment will obviously be made from a material which will keep out *all* forms of moisture. In effect, what this means is that it will not allow any moisture emanating from the body to escape, and the inevitable result is that body moisture (in the form of perspiration) will condense on the inside of the garment and make you wet. If you have never experienced this problem, you will be surprised how much moisture the body produces. If you do not believe me, try running round the garden wearing a bin liner!

These problems have largely been overcome by the advent of 'breathable' waterproof materials which allow the passage of water vapour whilst stopping water droplets (see next section) and these fabrics can serve the dual role of waterproof and windproof. The major problem with breathable fabrics is expense – particularly hard to justify for the 'casual walker'. However, you should consider the fact that one breathable waterproof garment can take the place of two more traditional garments, and may therefore be a fairly cost-effective purchase.

The traditional windproof garment is the **anorak**. This is usually made from one or more layers of a closely woven, cotton-based fabric, the best and most expensive being Ventile. Although many of these garments are water resistant, only a few are waterproof. This is an important difference.

Anoraks, or more modern walking jackets, should be long enough to cover the buttocks, and should have a large hood which comfortably covers your head even when you are wearing a hat. Some hoods are removable, being held in place by press studs. If you are choosing a jacket of this type, make sure the press studs offer a positive attachment and are positioned in such a way that you do not run the risk of getting a draught down the back of your neck. Other useful features include storm cuffs (i.e. elasticated inner-cuffs) and at least one zipped pocket which is large enough to hold a map.

Two basic styles of anorak are available. Those based on a jacket style should have full-length zips; the better and more expensive models having well covered (i.e. baffled), large-toothed, two-way zips and possibly an inner pocket which is accessible from behind the baffle. Such pockets are extremely useful because you can use them in bad weather without having to undo the jacket. Remember that an unbaffled zip will not present any barrier to the wind.

The other style of anorak is that in which the garment only has a half-length zip and must therefore be put on and taken off over the head. Although these are less convenient than the jacket styles (especially on steep ground in windy weather), they are no less effective, and the better ones will have a full, 'bellows-type' internal baffle behind the half-zip, and a large pouch pocket which is both baffled and zipped. Many also have drawstring waists and some form of crutch-strap.

Mention must be made of **waxed-cotton jackets**. Although these are ideal for general outdoor wear, being hard-wearing and functional, I find them far from ideal as walking jackets for a number of reasons, not the least of which is their weight. Whilst there is no reason to prevent you wearing such a jacket during your shorter walks, you will find them cumbersome and heavy if you intend to travel any distance. In any case, a good waxed-cotton jacket is not cheap, and you will almost certainly find something better suited to walking for the same price.

Finally, although it is possible to buy windproof **overtrousers**, they tend to be expensive and are of limited use to the casual walker. In any case, as we discussed in the last chapter, your walking trousers or breeches should be fairly wind resistant. If you do decide to buy some form of windproof overtrousers, I have no hesitation in recommending that you buy a pair made from a breathable waterproof fabric as described in the next section. These will not be that much more expensive than simple windproof overtrousers, yet will be far more cost effective as they will be waterproof as well.

Waterproofs

The two main problems faced when choosing waterproof shell garments are firstly that manufacturers appear to have different ideas about what constitutes a 'waterproof' material; and secondly that if a material really is 100 per cent waterproof, you will get wet from perspiration simply by wearing it – even on a dry day.

Most of the waterproof shell garments suitable for use when

walking are made from some form of proofed nylon material. The traditional garment is the 'cagoule', which can be likened to a long, lightweight nylon sack with arms and a hood. Designed to be used in conjunction with an anorak, the cagoule was considered an essential item of walking clothing for many years. Times have now changed, and jacket-style waterproofs are becoming far more common (and far more effective).

There are a number of basic design features for which you should look when choosing your shell garments. Assuming that they are made from some form of nylon material (and the vast majority will be), the proofing should be done either with neoprene or, preferably, polyurethane. Remember, both are coatings which will eventually wear away and, generally speaking, the lighter the fabric they proof, the quicker the coating will deteriorate. The lightest practical fabric for walking purposes is known as 2oz nylon, but I would advise you to choose something substantially heavier than this (i.e. 7oz) if you intend to walk regularly or go for anything more than the occasional Sunday afternoon stroll.

Waterproof jackets should be long enough to reach the base of the buttocks, and the front opening should be zipped, the zip being baffled to prevent the ingress of water through its teeth. Large-toothed zips are far superior to small-toothed zips, being more robust and less likely to jam. There should preferably be no seams across the shoulders (these are extremely weak and will soon leak no matter how well proofed they are initially), and any seams there are should either be sealed or, far better, 'hot-taped'. The jacket should have a hood which is large enough to accommodate a woolly hat, and which can be closed fairly tight via a drawstring. In this respect, it also helps to have a front zip which extends well up towards the mouth, but if, like me, you are bearded, make sure there is some form of 'beard-guard' or internal baffle. (From painful experience I can assure you that getting your beard trapped in a zip is something you would not wish to do twice!)

In addition to a jacket, you may well like to consider buying a pair of waterproof overtrousers. Indeed, these should be regarded as essential if you intend to do any mountain, moorland or long-distance walking. Waterproof overtrousers should be fairly roomy, and there should be some arrangement whereby you can put on the trousers without having to remove your boots. This usually takes the form of a zipped gusset extending from the base of the leg to the knee, although other methods have been tried. Whatever method is used, make sure it does not leak. They should also be fairly long in the leg, otherwise the water which runs down them will simply flow into the top of your boot. If this tends to happen anyway, the problem can be overcome by wearing gaiters (see next section).

One disadvantage of waterproof overtrousers made from standard waterproof fabrics is that they tend to be horrendously 'sticky' due to the problems of condensation mentioned below. For this reason, many have some form of mesh ventilation extending from the top of the thighs to the waist. There are two considerations here: firstly, make sure that the lowest part of the mesh lies well above the lowest part of your jacket! Secondly, the mesh itself lies under a waterproof covering (i.e. the jacket), so you should not expect it to be totally efficient.

The fact that walking, by its energetic nature, produces water vapour in the form of sweat can be a problem. The moisture usually travels through the insulating layers, eventually reaching the surface of the clothing and escaping. If your shell garment is 100 per cent waterproof the vapour will be unable to escape, and will condense on the inside of the barrier. Indeed, this process is extremely noticeable if you wear a waterproof on a warm but misty day, the end result often being that you get wetter through wearing the waterproof than would have been the case had you not worn it. However, it is better to wear this type of waterproof than none at all because it provides a barrier to evaporation. This means that, although you may get wet, the amount of heat loss will be reduced dramatically.

The only way around this problem is to choose shell garments which are made from one of the growing number of breathable waterproof materials, perhaps the best-known and best-tested being 'Goretex'. These materials are made in such a way that water vapour is allowed to pass through but water droplets are stopped, thus allowing body moisture to escape. The best of these materials are reasonably durable, and work extremely well in virtually all weather conditions. However, there are a few which are not so good, simply because they cannot stand up to the wear and tear of walking. In general terms, you get what you pay for – and the best is not cheap.

All the design features mentioned above should be present in breathable waterproof garments, and it should be noted that the only successful method of sealing seams in such fabrics is through hot-taping. Because these garments can be used successfully as both waterproofs and windproofs, there are several designs in which the best features of anoraks and waterproofs have been combined, but there are also several garments available which owe more to fashion than to function, and are therefore not really suitable for use by more serious walkers.

Protection for the extremities

Regardless of your various layers of clothing, without some form of protection, the hands and feet can get extremely cold, even in mild conditions, and especially if the walk takes place over any length of time. Additionally, an unprotected head can radiate up to 50 per cent of the body's heat.

The head is best protected by some form of woollen hat, either a simple woollen one or a woollen ski hat; a growing number of hill walkers are also wearing South American-style 'inca' hats with ear flaps. For particularly harsh weather, or demanding walks, a balaclava is useful. Brushed wool is ideal; alternatively, polypropylene, silk and thermal fleece are suitable materials. The more wind resistant balaclavas are, the better, although in particularly cold conditions they are often worn in conjunction with a walking jacket hood. ('Paramilitary' masks in which there are separate holes for the mouth and each eye are generally unsuitable for walking as they restrict the vision far too much.)

It is worth noting that you should also wear a hat in particularly hot and sunny weather. As its main task will be to protect your head and neck from the full force of the sun, it is best to wear one that is light in colour (preferably white), and made from a light-weight fabric – cotton being ideal. Because it also has to protect the neck, the hat should either have a fairly wide brim or should extend down the back of the head for some distance (like a legionnaire's hat). A (clean) white handkerchief draped from under the back of the hat will have the same effect.

For the hands, there can be little doubt that mittens are far superior to gloves. Wool, again, is a good material, although there are some excellent and very warm nylon mittens available which are lined with fibre-pile. Although these are not waterproof, they retain much of their warmth when wet, and many dry out fairly quickly. Waterproof thermal mittens are available (at a price), and you can also buy them made from breathable waterproof materials (at an even higher price).

Gloves are best made of wool although, again, it is possible to

11. Clothing should be functional, keeping the body 'core' and the extremities warm, dry and comfortable. More specialised clothing should be considered when walking in remote areas

buy nylon (and breathable) gloves lined with thermal material. Leather gloves are not to be recommended as they have surprisingly little insulation value, especially when they get wet. Very thin gloves made from polypropylene (thermal underwear material) are available, and these are excellent both for use by themselves and as liners for mittens on particularly cold days. They are also useful if you need to use your hands for any purpose (e.g. photography), as are fingerless woollen gloves.

Whatever you choose to wear, it is important that there should be no restriction of circulation. Restriction of movement is one thing (your mittens, for example, will undoubtedly be cumbersome), but restriction of the blood flow is another matter altogether. Apart from the fact that a lack of blood flowing to the hands or fingers will make them feel cold that much quicker, you also run the very real risk of frost-nip on particularly cold days (see Chapter 14).

Last but by no means least, are the feet. Whatever the weather, these are best protected by wearing at least one pair of thick woollen socks or stockings. The best of these will be constructed either entirely of 'loopstitch', or will have a 'loopstitch' foot together with a ribbed or standard knitted leg. The advantage of loopstich is that it both cushions and insulates. People with sensitive feet may find that they cannot stand heavyweight wool next to the skin. In this case thick woollen socks can be worn over the top of either thin socks of thermal material, or the type of sock you usually wear every day. The final number of socks you wear is entirely up to you; although most people seem to wear two pairs, I know of some people who wear only one pair, and others who wear three or more.

Finally, in really cold or wet conditions you might like to wear a pair of gaiters. These will help to prevent water or snow from entering your boots and, if you are not wearing overtrousers, will give your calves a certain amount of protection from the wind. Those made of canvas are good, durable, all-round gaiters which can be fairly successfully reproofed with a proprietary proofing compound; those made of nylon tend to make your legs feel sticky, are difficult to reproof, and can make a surprising and very annoying amount of noise. Gaiters made from breathable water-proof materials are horrendously expensive, and get so much wear and tear that they loose many of their properties within a remark-ably short space of time. Needless to say, I honestly do not think they are worth their price.

'Yeti' gaiters (which cover the whole boot), can be excellent, although their performance varies depending upon the type of boot. Certain types of boot have been designed to take certain types of Yeti gaiter, and these generally work together very well. You should enquire about the various combinations at your friendly local gear shop.

PART III

Equipment

6

Backpacks

Daysacks

There is little to beat the convenience of a small rucksack or 'daysack' for carrying light waterproofs, spare sweaters and so on. A well designed daysack leaves hands free, is reasonably waterproof and is far more comfortable than any form of shoulder bag or sports bag because the load is spread across both shoulders, generally on straps which are far wider and better padded.

A number of excellent daysacks are available at extremely competitive prices. When choosing a day sack, there are a number of factors which should be borne in mind.

Size

Having a daysack which is too large can be as much of a problem as one which is too small, primarily because of the temptation to fill the available space. It does not matter where you walk, nor for how long: weight is one of your biggest enemies and you should try not to encumber yourself with unnecessary objects.

The capacity of backpacks is generally quoted in 'litres', with capacities for daypacks ranging from 15 to about 50 litres. Obviously, the further you walk, the rougher the terrain or the more extreme the weather, the larger should be the capacity of your daysack, simply because you will need to carry more items of clothing and equipment. For strolling down country lanes and visiting the various types of waymarked trails, for example, you will generally need to take very little, and a 20 litre daysack will usually be more than adequate. When travelling further afield on less well-trodden paths, on the other hand, you might be better advised to choose a daysack with a capacity of between 20 and 30 litres. At the ultimate extreme, walking in remote areas under winter conditions may require the use of a daysack with a capacity of nearer 50 litres. (These capacities are based upon the assumption that everyone will carry their own daysack.)

For young children and family walks children's daysacks are available with capacities of between 5 and 15 litres. These will allow your child to carry his or her waterproof and perhaps some lunch.

Design

The more simple and straightforward the design the better. The main body of the daysack is best formed from a rectangular sack of a water-resistant or waterproof material. Nylon is ideal as it is hard-wearing and light, and although canvas and 'cordura' (a man-made, canvas-type fabric) are more durable, they suffer from the disadvantage that they are also heavier. All seams should be strongly sewn, and it is well worth checking the quality of the stitching as this varies considerably from manufacturer to manufacturer.

The top of the sack should be fitted with some form of draw-cord, and be covered with a large flap. In the better designs, this flap will be shaped and may have elasticated sides which enable it to fit snugly over the opening, thus keeping out the majority of any rain. However, whatever the claims made by the manufacturer, I have yet to come across any type of rucksack which is 100 per cent waterproof. Even if the material is waterproof, there are so many seams and stress points, plus the large opening at the top, that water is bound to seep in somewhere. I would therefore advise you to place anything you wish to keep dry in a plastic bag before packing it.

The shoulder straps should be attached firmly to the main body of the daysack, and should be well padded and at least 5 cm wide. They will obviously need to be adjustable, and this is best done via non-slip friction buckles which can be altered whilst on the move. You should aim to adjust the straps so that the load is carried as high as possible on your back, the weight bearing directly downwards. A light waist strap, although not essential, will certainly help to stabilise the daysack when walking across rough terrain and, in this instance, will do much to make the load more comfortable.

The way in which the straps are attached to the top of the daysack is very important, for if they are set too close there is a risk of them cutting into the base of your neck. For this reason, it is better to avoid daysacks which are shaped like a triangle, with narrow tops and wide bottoms. Furthermore, such daysacks are inefficient because they do not allow you to carry the load high on your back. A low load results in a bad posture in which you are bent forward, using back and shoulder muscles; a high load results in a straight posture in which the weight bears directly downwards onto the pelvic girdle, and thus onto the legs.

Long straps and large external pockets have an infuriating habit of becoming snagged in trees and brambles, etc., and you would do well to avoid those designs which are covered with pockets and huge lengths of webbing straps. However, one or two pockets can be useful for such things as drink flasks, nibbles, etc., and some of the better designed daysacks have compact side pockets, or a larger pouch pocket across the front of the daysack. Some form of pouch pocket can often be usefully incorporated into the top flap. For obvious reasons, all pockets should be zipped and baffled.

One of the problems you will have when carrying a rucksack for any length of time is that body moisture can build up where your back and the rucksack touch. This is particularly true if the rucksack is made of man-made materials. Although manufacturers have tried various ways of reducing this problem in their larger capacity rucksacks (see next section), only a few have gone to any length to do anything about it in their daysacks. The most common answer is to construct the sides and front of the sack from lightweight nylon fabric, whilst the back and base are made of canvas – a less-than 100 per cent effective solution, however.

Finally, those of you who only go on short strolls may well be interested to learn of 'bum-bags'. These are simply long, zipped pouch-pockets which fit snugly around your waist, and although designed originally for use by skiers, they are now commonly used by cyclists and have many applications for the more casual walker. The better models are certainly large enough to take a lightweight waterproof, and it may well be that you can use one of these instead of a daysack.

Backpacking rucksacks

A modern backpacking rucksack is a scientifically designed piece of equipment which should be chosen just as carefully as your boots. Indeed, the fit of the rucksack is of the utmost importance if it is to work at all efficiently. Needless to say, all the basic design features of a daysack should be present in a backpacking rucksack:

above all it should be simple in design and construction – and shaped in such a way that you are able to carry the load high on your back. Most importantly, of course, it should feel comfortable. Because you will be carrying a fair amount of weight, the rucksack itself should be as light as possible. However, there comes a point where the lighter-weight materials are not sufficiently durable to be particularly cost effective in the long term; and many backpacking rucksacks are constructed of fabrics of a similar weight to canvas or cordura. Whatever the material, beware of claims that the rucksack is waterproof – the material may be, but the rucksack will certainly not. One way of getting round the problem is to line the rucksack with a black plastic bin liner; alternatively, heavy-gauge polythene rucksack liners can be bought – more expensive but far more durable.

Size

The most popular models have a capacity of somewhere between 55 and 75 litres. In order to make do with a rucksack smaller than this, you will either have to be extremely efficient at packing or wealthy enough to afford a complete set of ultra-lightweight, ultra-compact equipment. On the other hand, if you consider you need a rucksack of larger than 75 litres, it might be worth checking whether your packing technique can be improved or whether all the items you are carrying are essential.

Design

Many backpacking rucksacks have two separate compartments, the upper one being accessible through the top flap in the normal way, the lower one being reached through a zipped opening, preferably using a two-way zip which is well baffled, which runs around the front and sides of the rucksack, usually about two-thirds of the way down. In some models, these two compartments are separated by a thin baffle which is also zipped and can therefore be removed. In others, the baffle is only attached at the front and the rear, and this means that long items such as tent poles can be carried inside the rucksack.

The most important difference between daysacks and backpacking rucksacks is the method by which the load is carried by the body. In a daysack, the shoulder straps do all the work; in the better backpacking rucksacks, on the other hand, some form of load-bearing hip-belt system ensures that the majority of the weight being carried is transferred directly onto the pelvic girdle.

This means that the main purpose of the shoulder straps is to keep the rucksack from falling backwards. One problem here is that because the shoulder straps can be worn quite loose, they can fairly easily slip from the shoulders. This can be annoying, and several models have some form of chest harness which allows you to clip the shoulder straps together across the chest, thus preventing them from slipping.

In order to work efficiently, both the shape of the rucksack and the position of the hip belt must be correct, hence the importance of a good fit. Not only should the back of the rucksack mirror the curvature of your spine, but also the hip belt should fit snugly across the top part of your hips, *not* around your waist (see Figure 6, page 29). Although many rucksacks are adjustable (to a greater or lesser extent), several come in a number of different back lengths, and it therefore goes without saying that you should always try on a backpacking rucksack before buying it.

The body-hugging fit of such rucksacks means that there can be problems from a build-up of body moisture across the back, and several manufacturers have incorporated some form of 'ribbing' across the back of the rucksack in an attempt to alleviate this. As with daysacks, such solutions are not always successful.

Finally, some backpacking rucksacks are equipped with a number of compression straps at either side, and this makes them far more adaptable. As was mentioned in the last section, no matter what capacity your rucksack, you will be tempted to fill it to the brim, and this can result in unnecessary weight. By using the compression straps, you can alter the size of your rucksack to suit the amount of gear you need to take. Indeed, some rucksacks are designed in such a way that they can be used as a backpacking rucksack (when fully extended) or as a mountain-walking or winter daysack (when fully compressed).

7

What to Carry

In this chapter we look briefly at the types of equipment most suitable for use by walkers of all descriptions. Camping equipment is discussed in Chapter 8, and full details of map and compass techniques will be found in Chapters 11 and 12.

Maps

Almost without exception, the best maps are those produced by the Ordnance Survey. For general walking, when following lanes, waymarked trails and the more well trodden footpaths in lowland areas, the Ordnance Survey Landranger series of maps (drawn at a scale of 1:50,000) is more than adequate. These are widely available, each sheet covers a large area and there is enough detail to allow you to find your way around without too much difficulty (especially if used in conjunction with a guidebook).

When following the less well trodden footpaths, planning your own routes, walking in remote moorlands or mountain areas, or following less well walked sections of either official or unofficial long-distance footpaths, the Ordnance Survey's Pathfinder or Outdoor Leisure series are recommended, both of which are mapped at a scale of 1:25,000 (i.e. 4 cm per kilometre or about two and a half inches to the mile). The Outdoor Leisure series are basically large Pathfinder sheets which have been specially compiled to cover some of the more popular areas. Do not make the mistake of thinking they are maps of the National Parks – not all the National Parks are covered by the Outdoor Leisure series.

Pathfinder and Outdoor Leisure maps give far more detail than the Landranger series but suffer from several disadvantages. Although the Outdoor Leisure series should be fairly widely available – especially in the area which they cover – the Pathfinder sheets are not so popular and may be difficult to obtain off the shelf. If visiting an obscure area, therefore, it may be wise to order such a map in advance rather than relying on picking up one when you arrive. Pathfinder sheets, too, cover only a small area (200 square kilometres) and, unless your walk lies in the centre of the area, it is easy to 'walk off the map'. This means you will sometimes have to carry more than one sheet with you and, apart from any other considerations, these maps are not cheap. (Murphy's Law dictates that, wherever you are in the country, you will always be situated on the edge of a map!)

All the maps – Landranger, Pathfinder, and Outdoor Leisure – show public rights of way, the routes shown being correct at the time the map was compiled. Mistakes are rare, but do occur. Where the 1:25,000 scale maps score over their smaller-scale companions is in terms of the amount of information that can be shown. (See Chapters 11 and 12.)

Map protection

Consulting large sheets of paper in wet and windy conditions does not help their preservation, and many a map has been ruined by a gust of wind on a stormy day. For this reason, you may like to invest in a map case of some description, the best type being light and compact, exactly the right size to take a double fold of an Ordnance Survey map, and with a sealable opening at the bottom so as to resist the entry of water for as long as possible.

There are two problems with map cases. The first is that you can only see a small section of the map at any one time. Not only does this mean you may have to remove the map at regular intervals in order to refold it, but you will also be restricted in your navigation because you will only be able to use those features which are shown on the part of the map you can see. The second problem is that the vast majority of map cases are designed to hang around your neck, and many people find them extremely annoying on a windy day when they appear to have a life of their own and try to strangle you.

It is, of course, possible to proof your map in a number of ways. Clear, self-adhesive plastic film (such as that used when covering books) can be useful in this respect although it does tend to crack along seams and corners after only a short time. A better method is to use one of the proprietary waterproofing compounds which are widely available from specialist outdoor shops. Although 'Texnik', in particular, is extremely good and does, in fact, also strengthen the map to a limited degree, this method of proofing does not protect against the stronger gusts of wind which can rip a map to shreds in a matter of seconds.

Compass

The standard 'button' or 'boy scout' compass is not really adequate, being of little use other than giving a rough idea of direction. What you need is an 'orienting compass' similar to that shown in the diagram on page 115. This is basically in two parts: the compass housing which contains the magnetic needle, and the base plate. As will be seen later, this type of compass is invaluable for it makes both calculating and following accurate bearings simplicity itself. When choosing such a compass, make sure that the base plate is at least 10 cm long – with anything less you may have problems calculating bearings.

Although the type of model shown in the photograph will be perfectly adequate for the vast majority of walking, if you visit remote or mountainous areas with any regularity you might like to consider buying one of the expensive, but remarkably accurate, optical sighting compasses, further details of which are given in Chapter 12.

First-aid and emergency items

Accidents can happen to anyone. Experience does not make it any harder to turn your ankle or catch yourself in hidden barbed wire, and even if you do not suffer an accident yourself, you never know when you might come across one. It therefore makes sense at the very least to have thought about what you would do in an emergency, and to have considered the various items of equipment which may or may not be useful.

One way of looking at emergency equipment is to think in terms of a sliding scale upon which a set of waterproofs represents one extreme, and a search and rescue helicopter, the other. The type of equipment you need to carry will depend upon the type of accident you are likely to meet, and this, in turn, will depend upon the type of terrain in which you intend to walk. There is little point, for example, in carrying an avalanche beacon during summer afternoon strolls along the Norfolk Coast Path; conversely, you would be wise to carry some form of spare clothing on all but

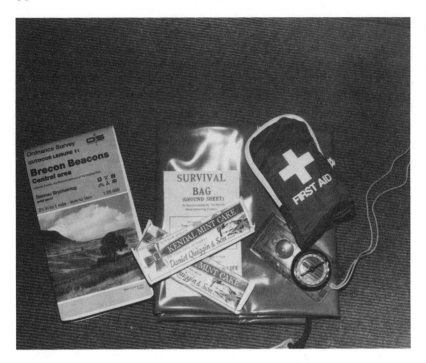

12. Essential equipment for more adventurous walks. Note map, compass, whistle, first aid kit, emergency food and survival bag. You will also need spare clothing and waterproofs etc.

the shortest of walks in the most settled of weather. Although a detailed discussion of specialist first-aid and emergency items is beyond the scope of this book, it will be useful to look at a few basics.

Your **spare clothing and waterproofs** can be thought of as representing the most basic form of emergency items. The further you walk, the more remote the area or the rougher the terrain, the more you will have to think about the type of spare clothing you intend to carry. Perhaps the best way to ensure that you have sufficient spare clothing with you during more demanding walks is to ask yourself whether you could survive a night in the open.

On all but the shortest of walks you would be wise to carry some form of **first-aid kit.** In its most basic form this may consist solely of a selection of plasters, possibly with the addition of a couple of bandages, a safety pin and a few aspirin. A far more comprehensive kit should be carried during mountain or moorland walking, and as a minimum this should contain triangular bandages, wound dressings, zinc oxide plaster, elasticated bandage etc., in addition to the items mentioned above. It is worth noting that most outdoor accidents are accompanied by a certain amount of blood, and a good first-aid kit will therefore contain a reasonable amount of absorbent material.

First aid is something which is sadly neglected in Britain. It is of little use carrying first-aid equipment if you do not know how to use it, and I would encourage you to attend a first-aid course if at all possible. Certainly, if you intend to walk with any regularity in rough terrain or in remote areas you should know (as a basic minimum) how to perform CPR (cardiopulmonary resuscitation); how and when to perform various forms of artificial respiration (including mouth-to-mouth and mouth-to-nose); how to stop severe bleeding; and how to place someone in the coma or recovery position. It is also essential to recognise the dangers associated with any injury to the chest, head, neck and spine; to understand the effects of severe pain and medical shock; and to know something of the causes and effects of mountain hypothermia.

Food and drink are discussed in more detail later in this chapter. However, it is worth noting here that it is a good idea to carry with you some form of emergency food on longer walks. This should take the form of high-energy foodstuffs like chocolate and glucose sweets, nuts and raisins, dextrose tablets, etc. Unfortunately, such sweet items tend to have an almost irresistable attraction during the longer or more strenuous walks, and there is always the temptation to raid them, the inevitable result being that you find them gone when you really need them. The only way I know around this problem is to place them in a plastic bag and seal them using a whole roll of sticky tape.

Another item which will be found extremely useful is a **survival bag**. This is simply a heavy-duty polythene sack about 1 m wide and 2 m long; 'double' versions are also available. Cheap to buy, and available from all good outdoor equipment shops, such survival bags could literally save your life. Although they can be used as an emergency shelter if you are caught by an unexpected rainstorm, their main use is to reduce heat loss during severe weather. If caught on a mountainside, for example, you should find as much shelter as you can, then crawl inside your survival bag, preferably insulating yourself from the ground in some way (e.g. sitting on your rucksack). Far more effective than the silver foil 'space blankets', your survival bag can be left permanently in the bottom of your rucksack along with your emergency food.

A **whistle** is another essential item of emergency equipment for mountain and moorland walking. If you find yourself in difficulties you can use the whistle to attract attention, either by using SOS (three short blasts followed by three long blasts followed by three more short blasts then a short silence) or, particularly in the more remote areas, by using the International Mountain Distress Signal (see page 146). Keep whistling at fairly regular intervals until you are located. If you have no whistle you can give either of these distress signals by using waves of a handkerchief, flashes of a torch, yells, screams and so on.

Depending upon the type of walking being undertaken, other items will be found useful or even essential in an emergency. These can be very specialised and/or are a matter of personal choice. If you intend to undertake more serious journeys you may like to consult one of the relevant books listed in Appendix IV.

Food

Walking regularly can give you a ravenous appetite, partly due to all that fresh air, but, more importantly, because you are exercising major muscle groups and will therefore be using a considerable amount of energy. It therefore goes almost without saying that food is a very important part of walking. Indeed, particularly during walking holidays or before and during unusually long or strenuous walks, eating the wrong type of food can have a noticeable effect upon your performance.

The easiest way to illustrate the importance of food is to look at a typical day during which you go for a long and fairly strenuous walk. By far the most important meal of the day is breakfast, preferably a good, old-fashioned, full English fry-up, since although we generally think of sugars and sweet things in general as being energy foods, it is, in fact, fat which contains the most energy. The problem with fats is that they take a long time to digest, and this means that the energy locked within them is not immediately available. You should therefore leave a good hour or more between finishing your breakfast and starting your walk.

One of the delights of rural rambling can be stopping for lunch at a country pub. However, you will probably find walking in the afternoon less pleasant or easy than in the morning – especially if the beer's good! This is because stopping for more than about fifteen minutes breaks the body's natural rhythm and this, in turn, can lead to a feeling of lethargy and a stiffening of the muscles. Far from refreshing you ready for the afternoon, a long rest is likely to make you feel tired. This is even more noticeable if you have consumed large quantities of food, for all your body's energy will be concentrating on digestion.

'Little and often' should be the rule of the day when walking. This means instead of stopping for an hour in the middle of the day and eating all your food, stopping for ten minutes every hour or so and having a quick nibble. Additionally, there is nothing to stop you munching the odd snack whilst you are walking. The best foodstuffs for use when on the move are those which contain a high proportion of carbohydrates (i.e. starches and sugars). Although, weight for weight, carbohydrates do not contain so much energy as fats, the energy they do contain is available for use by the body almost immediately. Sugars are somewhat more effective than starches in this respect, so your trail snacks (for consumption whilst on the move) should have a high sugar content.

Your evening meal will probably represent the main meal of the day. It should be substantial enough to replace any energy that has been used during the walk, and, preferably, be hot.

Your diet is particularly important if you are camping, or if you are intending to walk in mountainous terrain or across remote moorland. In situations such as these you are likely to expend – and should therefore aim to consume – at least 4000 kilocalories per day.

Drink

Many walkers underestimate the amount of liquid the body needs whilst on the move, and dehydration is a far more common complaint than most people realise. During mountain walking in temperate conditions, for example, you should aim to drink up to 4 litres of liquid per day, and considerably greater quantities may be needed if you are undertaking particularly strenuous walking or if the weather is very hot. A flask of some description should be regarded as an essential piece of equipment for all but the shortest of lowland walks. If this can be filled with a high-calorie drink, so much the better.

In very hot weather, some form of electrolyte (body salt) replacement drink will be found extremely useful (see also Chapter 7). Conversely, in very cold conditions, a hot drink can be a real boon and may even be a life saver in an emergency. Although expensive, unbreakable vacuum flasks are extremely useful in this respect. Strictly speaking, there will be no need to take a vacuum flask if you are camping, for you should have the necessary equipment and ingredients to make a brew 'in the field' (purists may like to make a brew in this way whether they are camping or not).

One final point worth noting is that, although a 'pub stop' can seem an attractive proposition, it is unwise to consume alcohol immediately before or during a walk. Apart from any other considerations, one of the effects of alcohol is to dilate the capilliaries (see Chapter 14), and this leads to increased heat loss. In simple terms, this means you are far more likely to suffer from hypothermia after having drunk even a small amount of alcohol. For similar reasons, you should never give alcohol to an injured walker; the brandy flask around the St Bernard's neck is more likely to kill the lost traveller than to save him!

Useful odds and ends

When it comes to 'extras', what some people might consider an indispensable item, others may find totally useless. Below are some suggestions for items that I have found useful during a variety of styles of walk.

First a **camera**. This need be neither bulky nor unwieldy. Some of the modern compact 35 mm models, for example, give excellent results, and if you wish to have more control (which usually means carrying an SLR camera), you will doubtless find zoom lenses particularly useful. I tend to do a fair amount of outdoor photography, and carry an SLR camera with two zoom lenses, one 28 mm to 85 mm, the other 75 mm to 210 mm, both with macro facilities.

Binoculars, too, can be extremely useful and, like cameras, have undergone something of a revolution during the past decade. Models are available which are no larger or heavier than the average personal stereo, yet which have excellent optics and a surprisingly clear image (or bright field of view). If weight and bulk are particularly important (as in a long backpacking trip) you may like to consider a small telescope or, perhaps better, a monocular.

Related to the above items, an **identification book** may be useful. (Remember not to pick a wild flower in order to identify it later – apart from any other considerations, you may well be committing an offence under the Wildlife and Countryside Acts.) Another item which many walkers consider to be indispensable is some form of 'sitmat', perhaps made from small rectangles of closed cell foam, similar to that used in the sleepmats mentioned in Chapter 8. (You could, of course, sit on your rucksack, thus doing away with the need to carry anything extra.)

Even if you are camping and are carrying a stove and cookset, a **vacuum flask** can be very convenient. No matter how careful you are, however, the standard, glass-lined flasks tend to have an annoying habit of breaking, and if you walk regularly, an unbreakable flask will be far more functional. The best such flasks are those made entirely from stainless steel. They are, however, fairly expensive.

Particularly in winter, when days are short and darkness can fall with surprising speed, it is a good idea to carry a **torch**. Indeed, if you are walking in the mountains or remote moorland areas, a reliable torch should be regarded as essential. Although there are a number of very bright, very durable hand torches available, the most useful type for our purposes is a head torch. Whatever the model, whatever the type, make sure that it cannot become turned on accidentally whilst in your rucksack. To be on the safe side, either insert the batteries incorrectly until you come to need the torch or, better still, keep the torch and batteries separate.

If you are camping, things like aluminium foil, plastic bags and paracord (thin nylon line) have countless uses; and a small sponge, perhaps with some form of scouring pad fixed to one side, is extremely helpful in clearing up the inevitable spills. A small knife is in my view, vital and it is far better to choose one with one sharp blade and, perhaps, a few functional tools than to go for an unwieldy monstrosity with countless blades which snap the first time you come to use them.

Other useful items include a spare pair of boot laces (which can be left permanently in the bottom of your rucksack) and, particularly if you have sensitive skin, it is not a bad idea to carry a small tube of sunscreen and some lipsalve. The main thing to remember is that weight is your enemy. So long as you always carry the items which are essential for the type of walking you intend to do, the odds and ends which may make your journey a little more comfortable (or even luxurious) are entirely a matter of personal preference.

8

Camping Equipment

Tents

There is something elegantly primitive and totally satisfying about the camping life, and this sense of satisfaction tends to increase, the further one goes from civilisation. However, the majority of tents are totally unsuitable for use when walking, unless, of course, you are working from a sheltered valley base camp to which you have transported all your equipment by car. You are not, for example, going to enjoy your walking if you are carrying a three-room frame-tent on your back!

Even if you are staying at low level, you would be well advised to consider only those tents designed specifically for backpacking use. Additionally, if you intend to camp in mountainous or high moorland areas, your tent may well have to take on the role of a piece of survival equipment, and you should therefore choose a model which has been developed for use in the type of harsh conditions which can be met in such terrain. However, even if you narrow down your choice purely to backpacking and mountain tents, you will still be faced with a vast range of differing models, each of which purports to be the best for the job.

Although a tent will represent only a fraction of the total weight you need to carry – food, cooking equipment, sleeping bag, clothing and so on occupying the remainder – it will probably be the heaviest single item. One of the major considerations when acquiring a tent is therefore weight. There are some excellent lightweight tents available, several of which are suitable for use by walkers. However, there are others in which the weight has been kept low by using materials which are less robust and durable than those used as standard, and these models would be unlikely to cope with the types of conditions to be found, for example, at a high-level, rocky site in a mountain region.

With the advent of flexible tent poles, tent designers have had something of a field day. Whereas, ten years ago, the standard design was that of the 'ridge tent', that familiar tent shape employing two upright poles (or two sets of 'A' poles) and a ridge pole, this is nowadays only one design out of many. In addition to several variations on this standard ridge design, such as sloping ridge tents and transverse ridge tents, there are wedge tents, tunnel tents, single hoop tents, crossover dome tents, geodesic dome tents and a whole host of other tents in which designers have tried, with varying degrees of success, to combine the best features of each basic shape.

Whilst the shape can have an effect on both the performance and the amount of material used (and therefore the weight), it is not, in itself, the most important consideration. No matter what the basic shape of the tent, there are certain features which it should possess if it is to be at all effective in protecting you from the elements. We have already said that it should be light; it should also be low in bulk because space is going to be at a premium. It will also help if it has been designed in such a way that it is relatively easy to pitch and strike (i.e. to put up and take down).

The weatherproof qualities of the tent will be enhanced if it is constructed of a double skin (see also below). This is normally done by having an inner compartment which is totally covered by an outer, all-round flysheet which reaches to within a few inches of the ground. This flysheet should be made from a totally waterproof material and should also cover the doors. The inner compartment, which should *not* be made from a waterproof material (for the reasons outlined below) should have a sewn-in groundsheet made from a fairly durable, 100 per cent waterproof material, and this should extend up the walls of the tent for at least 10 cm, thus creating a type of waterproof tray.

If the design is such that there is space between the inner tent and the flysheet in which to store wet gear, so much the better. Additionally, a porch extension or some other design which allows you to cook in the entrance to the tent but beneath the flysheet will be a boon in inclement conditions.

Many people assume that a tent made entirely from waterproof materials is far superior to one in which only the flysheet and the groundsheet are waterproof. Although such a design is fine in theory, it does not take into consideration condensation. If the inner tent is made from a material which is 100 per cent waterproof, water vapour from breath, hot drinks, cooking and so on will condense on the inside wall of the inner tent, the resulting moisture then running down to form pools on the groundsheet. If, on the other hand, the inner tent is made of a non-waterproof material, the vapour will pass through to condense harmlessly on the inner walls of the flysheet.

Another way around this problem is to use breathable waterproof materials such as Goretex™ which allow the water vapour to pass whilst stopping water droplets from entering. Tents made of these materials are extremely light because they need only be made from a single skin (i.e. there is no need for a flysheet). However, they are also extremely expensive, and they tend not to work well in the humid climate of Great Britain. That being said, there are some excellent and highly efficient one-person models available, and these may be found ideal if you like the idea of solo backpacking and are not claustrophobic!

A final consideration is that the further you camp from habitation or the rougher the terrain, the more important it becomes that your tent is stable enough to stand up to the worst of the weather. A tent which blows down in the teeth of a storm when you are miles away from habitation can land you in an extremely serious situation, and even if you are camped at a low-level valley site, your comfort is not going to be enhanced by water dripping through the roof all night. As it happens, most good-quality tents have some form of season rating ('one season', 'two season' and so on). If you intend to camp in the mountains or the more remote moorlands, you would be well advised to choose a tent with at least a four-season rating.

Sleeping bags

Although sleeping bags tend to be associated with camping, this need not always be the case. Indeed, you would be wise to consider the merits of carrying a sleeping bag when walking in any remote area in winter conditions, and many people – myself included – consider a good-quality sleeping bag to be an essential item of safety equipment when mountain walking in winter in such areas as the Cairngorms or the North-west Highlands of Scotland.

The main purpose of a sleeping bag is to keep you warm. It can be thought of as two sacks of fabric, one inside the other, with heat loss from inside the inner bag prevented by filling the gap in between the two sacks with some form of insulating material to trap the air. The type and amount of this filling determines the degree of heat loss that can be prevented, and hence the 'warmth' of the sleeping bag.

Sleeping-bag warmth is almost invariably quoted in terms of 'seasons', and the season rating of a sleeping bag will usually give you a fair idea of the type of conditions for which it was designed. Unfortunately, some manufacturers seem to have rather strange ideas about the types of temperature that can be met during the various seasons, and it is therefore advisable that you ask what is the lowest temperature for which any particular bag was designed before parting with any cash.

The season rating goes from two to five and, apart from the fifth season(!), is self explanatory. A two-season bag, for example, is suitable for use in late spring, summer and early autumn. A three-season bag is generally suitable for use in all but winter conditions, although the better-quality three-season bags may be suitable for winter use in valley sites. A four-season bag, by definition, is suitable for year-round use, but you should not forget that winter conditions in mountain areas can be severe. If you intend to camp at high level in the mountains during winter conditions, you would be better advised to choose a sleeping bag with a five-season rating.

There are almost as many different types of filling as there are different models of sleeping bag, but for the serious walker all but a few can be discounted. Kapok, for example, whilst being adequate for a summer caravanning bag, is totally unsuitable for outdoor camping; likewise, terylene fibres, although more effective, are generally far too heavy and bulky to be of any use to the backpacker.

Most of the synthetically filled sleeping bags suitable for use by walkers and backpackers will contain some form of hollow polyester fibres, the best of these being only fractionally inferior to the better natural fillings (see below). In some sleeping bags, the fibres will have been formed into layers known as 'batts', each batt being held together with resin. In other models, the fibres will be loose, and the sleeping bag will be described as having been 'blown filled'.

There are two main advantages to be gained by using hollow polyester fibres as a filling. Firstly, unlike sleeping bags with natural fillings, they retain many of their insulating properties when wet. Secondly, synthetic fillings are far cheaper! However, there are disadvantages as well, for such sleeping bags are always heavier and more bulky than similarly rated sleeping bags containing natural insulation, even though these differences may be minimal in the more expensive models.

Many people believe that the filling used in naturally filled sleeping bags is eiderdown. This is very rarely the case. Indeed, pure eiderdown has been virtually unobtainable for over forty years, and a good-quality, pure-eiderdown sleeping bag is nowadays worth a king's ransom. Most modern pure-down bags will be filled either with goose down (very expensive) or duck down (only slightly less expensive). Because of the price of down, sleeping bags using 'second-hand' or used duck-down fillings are not unknown, and many of these are not to be sneered at.

The least expensive (but still not cheap) of this type of sleeping bag will be filled with some form of down/feather mix. Generally speaking, the higher the percentage of down, the more efficient will be the insulation. One problem is that the quality of the feathers used can vary quite considerably, and this can have a marked effect not only on the performance of the sleeping bag, but also on its weight and bulk.

Apart from the price, the biggest single disadvantage with natural fillings is that they lose much of their insulating property if they get wet, the individual feathers clumping together in a soggy mass which can trap hardly any air at all. For this reason it is imperative that such sleeping bags are kept dry. Although the obvious way around this problem is to use a waterproof material for the fabric of the sleeping bag, the situation is complicated by the fact that the average adult loses a surprisingly large amount of body fluid every night in the form of vapour, and a waterproof fabric would therefore lead to condensation problems. Down-filled sleeping bags using breathable waterproof fabrics are available, but most people will need a very friendly bank manager if they wish to buy one.

Perhaps the easiest way to put some perspective on the differences between natural fillings and synthetic fillings is to say that, warmth for warmth, the best quality synthetic filled bags are slightly heavier, fractionally more bulky, but far less expensive than their down-filled counterparts. However, they do not transmit water vapour so well (and can therefore feel sticky), and they lack the luxurious softness of down.

The way in which the sleeping bag has been constructed is of

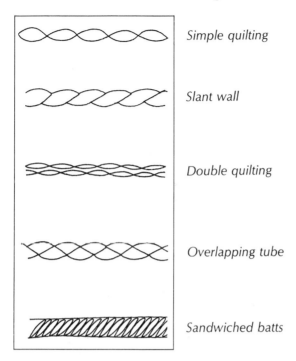

Simple quilting

Slant wall

Double quilting

Overlapping tube

Sandwiched batts

13. Sleeping bag construction

the utmost importance, particularly with natural and blown synthetic fillings. If the gap between the inner and outer sacks is not compartmentalised in some way, the filling is free to move around (or 'migrate'), and this will led to 'cold spots' where the filling is particularly thin or even totally absent. Although simple quilting (i.e. joining the inner and outer sacks with a line of stitches) will stop the migration, it is not effective because it causes cold spots along the seams. What is needed is some form of baffle, and the more common solutions are shown in Figure 13.

Sleeping bags should be stored out of their stuff sacks, preferably hanging vertically from a clothes hanger in the back of a wardrobe. Many have loops at the foot end to facilitate this. When you come to pack them ready for a journey, do not fold and roll them, but literally stuff them into their stuff sack, using compression straps if space is at a premium. They should be removed from the stuff sack, shaken out and left to loft up as soon as possible on arrival at a campsite. Additionally, they should be kept as clean as possible because no sleeping bag likes being washed, especially those with down fillings.

Finally, since the insulation in sleeping bags works on exactly the same principle as that in clothing – it traps air – when you lie down, you compress the filling, thereby reducing the amount of air, and thus reducing the insulation value. No matter how good your sleeping bag, you should carry something with which to insulate yourself from the ground, the most commonly used items being 'sleepmats' made from closed-cell foam. These sleepmats are widely available from outdoor gear shops, and it is worth shopping around as prices vary considerably. However, if you find what appears to be a bargain, do check to ensure that it is made of closed-cell foam as opposed to open-cell foam or else you will end up lying on a soggy sponge.

Stoves

A lightweight stove is essential for camping trips; in addition, many walkers like to carry one in preference to a vacuum flask. The rising popularity of all forms of outdoor leisure has resulted in the development of a vast range of lightweight stoves, not all of which are suitable for walkers. The easiest way to look at this range is to classify the stoves according to the fuel they use.

Solid-fuel and **jelly-fuel** stoves represent what could be considered as the bottom of the range. Cheap and cheerful, some of them are remarkably effective for their size, but few are efficient enough to be worthy of serious consideration for anything other than occasional lowland use in sheltered spots during warm weather.

Gas Stoves are available in a growing range of shapes and sizes, some of the more compact models coming complete with a pan in which they can be stored when not being used. These stoves can be split into those using non-resealable cartridges, and those using resealable cartridges. Of the two types, those using resealable cartridges are the more convenient as they can be dismantled, thus taking up less room in your rucksack. However, even if the stove is compact, the cylinders are bulky, and they may not be readily available in remote areas.

Many of these stoves are highly efficient, extremely clean and undeniably convenient, and they probably represent the most widely used form of heating in general walking and lowland camping. However, they do have several disadvantages. Not only are they very expensive to run, but they also tend to burn with an infuriatingly small flame once you have used up more than about two-thirds of the cylinder. They tend to blow out with frustrating regularity if there is even the slightest draught, and they do not like cold temperatures. Indeed, butane gas (the most common fuel) is impossible to light in temperatures of below $-1°C$, and although some cylinders are available filled with propane (or a butane/propane mix) which burns in slightly lower temperatures, gas stoves in general do not like cold weather.

Methylated spirits stoves are becoming increasingly popular. Although still available, the days of the old-fashioned but very effective 'picnic stove' are numbered, the better modern spirits stoves coming as a compact unit complete with nesting pans and an optional kettle. Superb for first-time buyers, they are efficient and fairly cheap to run, and are the only types of stove which thrive on draughts. On the negative side, the fuel is heavy and burns surprisingly quickly, and this means that not only does the stove have to be refuelled regularly, but you also have to carry a fair amount of fuel with you if you are camping. Refuelling, too, can have its problems as methylated spirits burns with an almost invisible flame, and accidents can result if people try to refill a stove which is still alight.

For our purposes, paraffin and petrol stoves can be combined under the title, **pressure stoves**, although there are several important differences. It is essential to realise that the fuels are not interchangeable except in certain very specific models, these being described as multi-fuel stoves. Indeed, some of the multi-fuel stoves claim to burn any liquid fuel from diesel oil to vodka! Pressure stoves in general are probably the most widely used form of heating in mountain walking and 'wild country' camping. They are highly efficient, extremely economical and usually have a stupendous heat output. However, they are also relatively heavy, most models are bulky and all are very expensive to buy. Furthermore, all but a very few require priming (pre-heating the burner). Not only is this inconvenient, but it is also potentially very dangerous if done incorrectly, especially if you are using the stove when camping. A badly primed pressure stove is likely to 'flare', and when this happens, a fountain of burning liquid fuel sprays out of the burner, the flames sometimes reaching well over a metre. It is vitally important, therefore, that you read the instructions that come with the stove before attempting to light it for the first time, and that you are totally familiar with the lighting procedures before you use it on a camping trip.

If you are using a methylated spirits stove or a pressure stove you will need something in which to carry the liquid fuel. Methy-lated spirits, in particular, tends to creep, and will seek out and exploit even the slightest crack or weakness in a container. You should therefore only carry methylated spirits in a specially de-signed fuel bottle with a deeply threaded cap, and it is good practice to use such bottles no matter what liquid fuel you carry. The best of these fuel bottles are made of lightweight aluminium or aluminium alloy, and have replaceable sealing washers, option-al safety pouring tops and so on. Never use your fuel bottle for water or your water bottle for fuel.

You will also need something with which to light your stove. A cigarette lighter is extremely useful (whether you smoke or not), although you should carry spare flints and refuel it before each trip (not so much of a problem if you have a petrol lighter and a petrol stove). Matches are okay so long as you keep them dry; 'lifeboat matches' (which should, by rights, be both waterproof and wind-proof) are better but so expensive that they are best kept for those occasions when all else fails.

Cooksets

Unless you have bought a modern methylated spirits stove which is designed as a unit with nesting pans, or a compact gas stove which comes complete with a pan in which it can be stored, you will need something in which to make your brew or cook your food. If you intend to use your stove only to make the occasional brew, a small aluminium camping kettle will be ideal. These are available in several styles and sizes, the better ones having a folding handle which makes them less bulky and easier to pack in a small daysack. Certain models come equipped with a screw cap which fits over the spout, thus allowing them to be used as water carriers. If you choose one of these models, check the seal on the screw cap carefully as some types are renowned for leaking.

You will also need something from which to drink your brew, the most popular items being lightweight, unbreakable plastic mugs which are both practical and cheap. In very cold weather, some people like to carry an insulated mug, the disadvantage being that several of the most commonly available models are both heavy and surprisingly brittle.

For general outdoor cooking there are three main styles of cooking utensil to choose between: army-style mess tins, nesting billy cans (or dixies) and camping cooksets.

Mess tins are rectangular aluminium pans with folding handles, usually bought in pairs in which the smaller of the tins is the right size to fit into the larger. Indeed, the better ones nest so snugly that you can use them for storing food during transit. They are sturdy, simple and fairly adaptable (you can use them separately, as one pan with a lid or as plates and bowls), and are usually reasonably priced.

Billy cans, or 'billies', are available either singly or in nesting sets, and consist of an aluminium 'paint-pot' style can with a folding wire handle (usually removable), together with a deep lid which can double as a bowl or another small pan. This lid, too, usually comes with some form of folding handle. At the time of writing, billy cans are sold according to their (imperial) diameter, the smallest one generally available being the 5-inch. Nesting sets usually contain three cans with lids, these generally being between 5 and 7 inches in diameter, the lid of the 7-inch can doubling as a frying pan. Very much larger sizes are available. Indeed, billy cans, in general, tend to be more popular with groups than with individuals because they come in a wide range of sizes suitable for group catering.

The most popular form of cooking utensil for general outdoor use is the **cookset**. Like billy cans, these are available in a number of sizes; unlike billy cans, different sets have been designed specifically for different numbers of people and will be described as being suitable for one person (often called solo sets), two persons and so on. The contents of each cookset vary not only from size to size, but also from model to model, and you would be wise to check what is included as some are far more comprehensive than others. There will usually be one or more cooking pans with lids; a frying pan; a metal bowl or deep plate; and an adjustable handle which fits all the utensils. Some cooksets come complete with metal mugs, others include small kettles; the final choice is yours.

With regard to materials, most cooksets are made from aluminium or some form of aluminium alloy. This is light, fairly durable and reasonably priced. However, it is also possible to buy excellent cooksets made from high-quality stainless steel in which one or more of the cooking pans have copper bottoms. Although somewhat more expensive than those made from aluminium, these copper-bottomed stainless steel cooksets are highly recommended; they are far more durable, transmit the valuable heat from your stove far more evenly and will delight even the most fastidious of gourmet chefs.

14. *Cooking equipment. From left to right: spirits stove, cookset, gas stove with non-resealable cartridge, petrol pressure stove, gas stove with resealable cartridge, paraffin stove*

When it comes to eating, you may consider eating straight from the pan (thus keeping weight to a minimum); alternatively, you may like to take some form of plate with you. The most practical items are those made from unbreakable plastic, some form of deep plate being the most adaptable. This can be used for every course of every meal – as a cereal bowl, soup bowl, dinner plate and dessert dish.

For cutlery, plastic may be fine, but it has the unfortunate habit of breaking. On the other hand, standard kitchen cutlery, although durable, is remarkably heavy. The best idea here is to carry a cutlery 'clip set'. These are fairly durable and reasonably cheap, are generally made from some form of lightweight aluminium alloy, and usually contain a knife, fork and dessert spoon which can be clipped together during transit.

Part IV

TECHNIQUES

9

Planning and Preparation

Although I would be the last person to suggest that you should plan and prepare for each and every walk, there are times when some form of planning and preparation is desirable. Indeed, on the longer or more adventurous trips this is likely to be essential, particularly when visiting an area for the first time.

I would like to make a distinction between planning, on the one hand, and preparation on the other. Planning is simply working out where you are going to go, either generally or in detail, and may also include such things as booking accommodation, getting permission to camp in certain areas and so on. Preparation is more personal, and involves such things as checking to ensure that you have the necessary clothing and equipment, and that all this gear is serviceable. For longer or more strenuous trips, it may also include getting fit.

Planning

In its most basic form, planning will amount simply to looking at a map in order to choose an area in which to walk. Although many regular Sunday afternoon strollers will visit the same local area time and time again, many will take an occasional glance at a map to see if there is anywhere else nearby where they might pass a pleasant few hours. Indeed, it is a truism that one never knows what's on one's back doorstep, and I would encourage all walkers to buy a copy of the Ordnance Survey map of their local area; I can almost guarantee that they will find somewhere new to visit.

Guidebooks, too, can be of great help, even if you do not stray far from your front door. In the better of these, the basic research has been done for you, and whilst I would not suggest that all your walking should be done by following other people's preferences, a good guidebook will enable you to get to know the bare bones of an area. In any event, you can always fill in the details at a later date, should you so wish.

When you are intending to travel further afield, possibly for a few days, some form of planning becomes essential. Again, maps and guidebooks make ideal reference sources, and if you are visiting a popular area, particularly within a National Park, you will generally find that there is a wealth of information which you can obtain in advance. This will include such things as places to visit, various types of accommodation, details of local campsites and so on.

On longer trips, such as when backpacking along a long-distance footpath, you would be well advised to work out some form of daily itinerary so that, at the least, you have some idea of where you are going to spend each night. This is particularly important if you are following a popular path in the height of the season, when it may be prudent to pre-book your accommodation.

A further consideration is that of weather conditions. Particularly in mountain and remote moorland areas, you may well find that the conditions are such that it is inadvisable to follow certain routes, in which case you would be wise to have a few alternatives in mind. Dependence on the weather is, of course, a strong argument against planning your walks in detail too early, and many people will arrive in an area with only a rough idea of what they would like to do. Bearing this in mind, perhaps the best time to plan specific routes is the night before you intend to follow them, by which time you should have a good idea of the local conditions and the weather forecast.

When visiting more remote areas, it is a good idea to write down a few details of your proposed walk and leave these with a responsible person who can then alert the rescue services if you fail to return. Such 'route cards' should also give information about the number and ages of people in the party and the estimated time of return. They should also give some indication of any routes you might take to escape from bad weather. If you leave a route card with someone, it is imperative that you let them know when you return, otherwise a rescue team may be called out needlessly. (Note, also, that it is unwise to leave a route card on the window of your car – it is an open invitation to thieves.)

Route cards can also be of great use if you are caught in unexpectedly severe conditions, particularly if they give details of compass bearings, distances between definite features, rough timings and so on. It is far easier to work out such things in comfort the night before than in the teeth of a storm. Full details of route

15. Even the simplest of mountain walks can take you into spectacular scenery. But always make sure you are equipped for the walk you plan to do

card construction are beyond the scope of this book, but further information will be found in my book, *Mountain Navigation Techniques* (see Appendix IV).

Preparation

Preparation may consist simply of throwing a few things into a rucksack. However, particularly on longer walks, it is a good idea to ensure (perhaps by means of a checklist) that you have packed the essentials, and that everything is serviceable. The standard example of a lack of preparation is the bootlace which breaks within a few hundred yards of the start of the walk. After a while, preparation becomes a matter of routine, and you will find yourself checking kit almost subconsciously.

Finally, it is of little use starting out on a walk unless your body is prepared. You do not have to be super fit, but you should at least be capable, both physically and mentally, of completing the journey without too much suffering. If you are new to walking, you would be well advised to leave the longer and more adventurous trips until you are both fit and experienced enough to enjoy them.

10

Walking
Techniques

The techniques mentioned in this section really come into their own on the longer, more demanding walks where conservation of energy is a prime consideration. However, walking the correct way even in supposedly easy terrain will certainly help to make the experience more enjoyable, for you will feel fresher and more secure on your feet.

Uphill

The basic technique of a regular, rhythmic pace is a major factor in successful and enjoyable walking, particularly over long distances. Once you have found your rhythm, the body takes over, leaving the mind to wander at will and enjoy the surroundings. This same rhythm should be employed whether you are walking uphill or down, across a slope or along the flat, and there are only a few occasions when your rhythm need be broken (see section on Scrambling). Children, in particular, will find this very hard to do, as they tend to rush around at the start, striding out, full of energy, gradually getting slower and slower as the walk progresses.

Once you have tried this basic technique a few times, you will quickly begin to see that those people who slow down when walking uphill are going about it in totally the wrong way. Instead of altering your rhythm, you should shorten your stride, covering a smaller distance with each step. Place your feet carefully and firmly on the ground, and if you are not following a path, look ahead and plan your route in advance.

As the ground steepens still further, shorten your stride even more, and resist the temptation to 'edge' your boots. Instead, place the whole of the sole of the boot flat on the ground (even if this means flexing your ankles), and push up with your thighs rather than springing up from your calves. Each time you step up, push the knee back slightly to lock your leg and reduce the muscular effort.

Once the slope steepens above a certain angle, you will probably find it easier to zig-zag in an ascending traverse backwards and forwards across the slope. There is no hard-and-fast rule here; the exact angle at which you begin to zig-zag will vary from person to person and from slope to slope, as will the length of the zigs and the zags. You should still be planning your route in advance, looking not only for secure foot placements, but also for areas of slightly more level ground where it will be easy to change direction. Use all the local features you can to give your foot more support. No slope is totally smooth; there are always slight hummocks and indentations which can be used.

On particularly steep ground, one commonly sees people leaning into the slope. Unfortunately, although this is a natural thing to do, it is totally wrong, for it alters the body's centre of gravity and makes it far more likely that you will slip. What you should try to do is stand upright, even pushing away from the slope with your hands, if necessary. On no account should you pull yourself into the slope with your hands for the resultant forces will commonly result in your feet flying away from under you.

Never venture onto steep, rocky ground unless you have had some experience of rock climbing or scrambling (see later). Mistakes are easy to make and the consequences of a slip could be severe. Always ask yourself what might be the outcome of a slip before venturing onto anything but the most gentle of grassy slopes.

On rocky slopes, or slopes where there are loose rocks above, keep your eyes and ears open for falling stones. If you hear the cry 'Below!', don't look up unless the cry is from a very long way away, otherwise you risk getting a boulder in the face. If you dislodge a rock, bellow 'Below!' at the top of your voice, even if you cannot see anyone in the near vicinity.

When in a group ascending a scree slope (a slope composed of loose rocks), avoid following in each others' footsteps as any dislodged rocks will fall straight onto the person behind. In this situation it is far better to ascend in a line abreast or in an arrowhead formation so that the chance of dislodging a rock directly onto a companion is minimal.

In winter, even the easiest slopes of summer can become

treacherous and you would be well advised to avoid them whenever possible. Particularly in mountain areas, you should not attempt to ascend steep, snow-covered slopes unless you have at least some experience of snow- and ice-climbing techniques. Additionally, you should have an ice axe with you – assuming, of course, that you know how to use it.

Downhill

The mistake commonly made when descending slopes is that of lengthening stride. This is easy to do, yet is the quickest way to damage knees and destroy knee cartilage. The correct technique is in fact similar to that used when walking uphill. As the ground starts to drop away in front of you, keep to the same rhythm, shorten your stride, and place your feet flat on the ground, making use of any irregularities of slope to give you more purchase and security. On steeper slopes, you may prefer to zig-zag, in which case, here again, you should work out your route in advance, making use of platforms or other steps on which to change direction. Resist the temptation to descend directly by digging in your heels, particularly if you are wearing a pair of modern lightweight boots with cut-away heel sections.

Another common mistake is to descend with straight legs, with knees locked. This puts a huge strain on knees and cartilages, and is virtually guaranteed to cause problems after only a short while. Far better to descend with the legs slightly bent, using the large muscles of the thigh and calf as a form of shock absorber.

For fairly obvious reasons you should never run down steep slopes. Although it may be permissible to take very small, quick steps on short, steep, downhill sections, it is far better to keep to your rhythm all the time. Apart from the ever-present risk of knee damage, your head has a long way to go before it hits the ground if you fall, and if you put out your arms to save you, you are more than likely to break something, wrists, shoulders and collarbones being the most common. Additionally, you are likely to be totally out of control if you run, especially if you are wearing a heavy rucksack. I once watched with horror as a group of about six heavily laden youths ran headlong into a barbed wire fence at the bottom of a steep slope simply because they found it impossible to stop in time.

On particularly steep slopes you may well find it tempting to lean back slightly. As with leaning into the slope when ascending,

16. Mountain walking can require steady footwork. If the slope is really steep you might try zig-zagging, but never run down!

this is totally wrong, and will soon result in your feet sliding out from under you. If you constantly and suddenly sit down every time you descend a slope, it is probably due to the fact that you are unconsciously leaning backwards, albeit only slightly. (It is, of course, preferable to do this than to overcompensate, lean too far forward, and end up somersaulting down the slope.)

Exactly the same considerations apply when descending rocky slopes and scree slopes as when ascending them. Because of the danger of dislodging material onto your companions, you should descend in a line abreast or an arrowhead formation. One school of thought advocates descending with the apex pointing uphill, for if it points downhill, the person at the front stands twice as much chance of getting hit by a stone than anyone else. (Stones falling down slopes seem to follow routes of their own choosing, and can move a surprising distance sideways.)

One extra technique that can be used when descending certain scree slopes is that of scree running. Although this is exhilarating, it can also be extremely dangerous, and it is important that you bear several factors in mind before attempting it. First and foremost, you must be able to see *all* of the slope down which you intend to travel. This will be impossible if the visibility is poor or if it is nearing dusk, and there may be a drop camouflaged by the similarity in stones above and below it. Generally speaking, it is unwise to run down a scree slope which you have not already ascended. Second, the slope itself must be composed of rocks which are fairly small and uniform in size. Do not run slopes which have large islands of rock in them, or where there are large boulders perched on the scree.

The basic technique is to take a large step onto the scree, digging the heels well back, at which time the stones will start to move downwards. Now move the other leg, digging the heel well back again, and continuing walking as if descending an escalator. It is possible to gain quite a speed, your rate of descent being equal to that of your paces plus the speed of descent of the stones. When you want to stop, take a little jump, and dig both heels well back. Keep as upright as you can. If you lean too far back, you will end up sitting down but still moving (not a pleasant experience); if you lean too far forward you will somersault face first into the rocks below (an even less pleasant experience).

Two further points are worth noting. First, on all but ideal scree slopes, you should be wary of dislodging stones onto your companions (it may be advisable to descend such slopes one at a time). Second, scree running tends to drastically reduce the life of lightweight boots.

Descending more solid rocky slopes is something which should not be attempted lightly. Even on the easiest of ground it is more akin to scrambling than walking, for distances can be deceptive, and drops difficult to judge, especially in poor visibility or near dusk. Unless you are a rock climber, I would advise you to avoid all such unplanned descents wherever possible and, even if you are, never descend a section which you cannot easily reclimb.

Finally, descending snow slopes should be done with the utmost of care, and then only if you are sure that you can see the whole slope. As mentioned in the previous section, you should not be in the mountains when there is snow around unless you have an ice axe and know how to use it. It is worth remembering that the vast majority of winter accidents in the hills and mountains are caused initially by simple slips on easy ground.

Traversing slopes

When traversing slopes, you should bear in mind all the factors mentioned in the previous two sections. For example, one of the more common mistakes made by people unused to walking on steep terrain is to hold onto objects upslope of them, the inevitable result being that they lean into the slope. As we have seen, this alters the body's centre of gravity and puts an 'outward' pressure on the feet, making them far more likely to slip. It is far better, in this situation, to push away from the slope, keeping the body weight directly over the feet. Generally speaking, it will be better for you to avoid all slopes which are steep enough for you to touch the ground by extending your arm horizontally, unless, of course, you are at the bottom of such slopes or this is simply a local steepening.

Another common mistake, similar again to those made during ascent and descent, is that of 'edging' the boots – placing the feet in such a way that only a small part of the sole touches the ground. You will be far more secure if you try to work out your route in advance, looking for places where you can get support for the feet, and placing them flat on the ground. Where this is not possible, try to flex your ankles in order to get as much of the sole of the boot on the ground as possible, thereby maximising the amount of friction.

There is a natural tendency to lose height when traversing, no matter how steep or otherwise the angle of the slope. The problem is that most people, once they realise this tendency, tend to over-compensate and gain height instead. This is particularly noticeable on both featureless and fairly smooth grassy slopes where there are few obvious reference points, and on scree or other slopes with a loose surface where you are constantly fighting to avoid slipping downhill! If it is important to stay at a particular level, you can reduce the potential error very effectively if you plan your route between objects or features which are on a similar

17. *Coastal walking for the more adventurous – on the Gower Peninsular in South Wales. You should never venture onto steep, rocky slopes unless you have had some experience of rock climbing or scrambling*

level to yourself and which are easily recognisable, assuming, of course, that visibility is sufficiently good.

Long, level traverses across steep, rough slopes can be particularly tiring on the ankles, and you may well find it preferable to plan your route in such a way that you walk along the top or bottom of the slope, or follow an ascending or descending traverse line.

Rough terrain

Whether your walking preferences are for something quite adventurous or for more or less well trodden footpaths, you will inevitably be faced with the occasional 'difficult' section. For instance, many of the more well used paths in popular areas now suffer badly from erosion, and this can lead to rough, loose surfaces, even where attempts have been made to rectify the problem. Whatever the conditions underfoot, when walking in a group make sure you give one another room to move, thus avoiding treading on each other's heels; and on a path which is only wide enough for one person, don't try to walk side by side!

If you find yourself on a badly eroded path, shorten your stride and place your feet carefully and deliberately, avoiding, wherever possible, edges which may crumble or cobbles which may roll. On badly maintained paths where there is overhanging vegetation, be careful not to let branches and twigs spring back into the face of the person immediately behind you, and do not forget that if you are forced to walk through high bracken, not only may you disturb hordes of marauding insects, but you may also get extremely wet if there has been any rainfall within the preceding few days. If the bracken is thick (as it often is) it will also obscure the ground, making it impossible to see where you are placing your feet.

Away from footpaths you may encounter a number of potential problems. Short, sheep-cropped grass can be surprisingly slippery when either very wet or very dry; long grass and heather may catch your feet and drag at your ankles; and tussocks and clumps of vegetation such as bilberry can destroy your rhythm and balance. Travelling through such terrain can therefore be surprisingly strenuous, particularly when walking across heath or moorland areas. Sometimes, following sheep-tracks (or similar) can be helpful, even though this may result in a zig-zag course.

Another problem common in moorland areas is that of bog. Contrary to popular opinion, there are few really dangerous areas of bog in Britain. If faced with boggy ground, try to search out the drier areas (often indicated by patches of heather). Tread carefully and deliberately (testing the solidity of the ground first, if necessary) and resist the temptation to leap from tussock to tussock, no matter how solid they may appear, unless you want a boot full of foul-smelling ooze – or a turned ankle.

In a previous section we touched upon some of the problems which can be met when moving on scree slopes. Level areas composed of loose stones or rocks can present equally difficult terrain. Boulder fields – areas of more or less level ground composed of loose rocks varying from pebbles to boulders the size of houses – are not uncommon in many upland areas, and you should always tread warily when struggling across them. Apart from the obvious hazard of slipping and damaging an ankle in a crevice, many apparently solid rocks will be loose and may move when you put your weight on them. Never leap from boulder to boulder – you are asking for trouble if you do so.

Even on more solid rocky terrain, treat all sloping surfaces with suspicion, particularly if the rock is at all mossy or wet. A rock may appear to provide a firm footing, but such surfaces can be extremely greasy and it is all too easy to slip. This is particularly true of surfaces which lie in the shade of exceptionally large boulders, under trees or beneath muddy and vegetated banks.

One of the most difficult and tiring types of terrain in which to walk is that in which bouldery or rocky ground is partially covered with vegetation. The problem is that you never know whether the rock is solid beneath the vegetation or whether there is a hidden crevice or a balanced boulder. Generally speaking, you would be wise to give such areas a wide berth whenever there is a suitable alternative, certainly until you have gained a fair amount of experience of walking across other forms of difficult terrain.

Worthy of passing mention are old industrial areas such as can be found in many mountain and moorland areas. Old mines and quarries, in particular, can be extremely hazardous, with unstable cliffs, hidden shafts and crumbling masonry. Stay away from all such areas, especially if you are walking with young children.

Finally, do not forget that the weather can have a marked effect on the terrain, the most obvious example being that snow and ice will make most surfaces extremely slippery. However, rain, too, can have almost as marked an effect, especially on hard-packed ground after a prolonged dry period, where it may result in a thin and highly slippery layer of mud. If you are at all worried about conditions underfoot, especially if you find yourself in a position such as at the top of steep ground where a slip might have serious consequences, ensure that you place your feet carefully in such a way that they get maximum support, and that you try to keep your body weight directly over your feet.

Scrambling

Where rocky ground is so steep that it requires you to use your hands as well as your feet in order to proceed with any degree of safety a special technique is required. This has more to do with rock climbing than with general walking and is called scrambling. However, if you decide to walk in the mountains on anything but the odd occasion, you may well find yourself in a position where a knowledge of the basic techniques of scrambling will be useful, if only to get yourself out of trouble.

It would be negligent of me not to emphasise the potential dangers of scrambling. When moving on rocky ground, particularly when going upwards, not only can you get yourself into a position where you are above some big drops, often before you realise the seriousness of your situation, but even a minor slip from no great a height can result in considerable pain, for the ground on which you land will almost inevitably be hard and unforgiving. If you land on bouldery ground, even after a fall of only a couple of feet or so, you are likely to injure yourself, possibly seriously. Bearing this in mind, if you like the sound of scrambling, I would advise you to go on a basic rock-climbing course (as offered by some of the organisations mentioned in Appendix III), or, at least, to start out in the company of someone more experienced than yourself.

The techniques used in scrambling can be thought of as being an extension of the techniques used in walking uphill. You should, for example, try to move steadily, pushing yourself up with your feet rather than pulling yourself up with your hands. It is good practice to try and keep your hands at, or slightly below, shoulder height, for in this way your body will be more upright, you will be able to see your footholds far more easily, and your weight will be directly over your feet.

A number of mistakes are commonly made by people when scrambling, the worst of which is reaching too high for a hand-hold. This inevitably results in the body being pulled into the rock, which is similar to, and as bad as, leaning into the slope when walking uphill, for it puts an outward pressure on the feet and makes you far more likely to slip.

Another common mistake is rushing to get to the top of a section of rock in the fastest possible time. Far better to stop near the bottom and work out the route you intend to take, only then moving steadily and deliberately, placing your feet carefully and testing the solidity of each hold before committing your full weight to it. Move one limb at a time so that you always have three points of contact with the rock (for example, two feet and one hand, or two hands and one foot), and *never* leap or lunge for a hold – it may not be as solid as you thought. If you find a doubtful hold, climb back down and see if you can work out another line of ascent.

If you come across loose rocks lying on a ledge, warn any companions who will be following you, then pass them by carefully. Even if you can see no one below you, resist the temptation to throw rocks down the cliff as there may be other people in the area hidden from view. You should ensure that your companions move well away from the line of any dislodged stones before you start to ascend, but, even then, should you accidentally dislodge any rocks, warn other people by shouting 'Below!' As mentioned earlier, if you hear someone shout this warning, do not look up.

You should never scramble up a piece of rock unless you are certain that you can also descend it. To do otherwise is a sure recipe for becoming cragfast. If you bear this and the above points in mind, you should be able to reach your destination without too many problems, but if you do find that it is difficult to proceed, or if you find that you are worried about a particular move, you should also be able to retreat to safety. Indeed, if you do come across problems, it is far better to scramble back down and try to plan a different route from the safety of more level ground than to hang about on steep rock getting increasingly tired and worried.

As was mentioned in the previous section, it is one thing scrambling up a section of cliff, but it is an entirely different matter scrambling down, especially if you have not passed that section before, and even more so if the visibility is poor. In conditions where the light is low, such as will be common not only at dusk but also on heavily overcast days or in misty conditions, you will find it almost impossible to judge depth and distance, and what may look like a drop of a few feet may well turn out to be more like ten or twenty. Avoid scrambling down in such conditions whenever possible, it is far safer to find a more level way around, even if this results in a considerable increase in distance. If, for some reason, you are forced to scramble down, make sure you keep your hands well below shoulder level, look down to see where you are going as opposed to feeling for holds, and never drop onto a ledge. Not only may you slip or the ledge give way, but there is also no guarantee that you will be able to continue, and you may not be able to get back.

Winter walking

Walking in winter conditions can be exhilarating, with landscapes transformed by a sprinkling of snow or a heavy coating of hoar frost, taking on a breathtaking, almost mystical, beauty.

The techniques of winter walking in mountain and moorland areas are beyond the scope of this book. Suffice it to say that if the mountains are clothed in snow and ice, you should not even consider venturing onto their slopes unless you are carrying an ice axe and, far more important, know how to use it. The most important use of the ice axe is not, as many people appear to think, to cut steps, but to prevent a slip from becoming a fall.

A further consideration is that winter days can be very short, especially in Scotland. Additionally, conditions underfoot may slow you down considerably. You should therefore plan your walks very carefully, allowing more than ample time to complete the journey, for otherwise you may run the risk of benightment. It is not being over-dramatic to say that the chances of surviving an unplanned night in the open on the Scottish hills in winter are minimal.

If you do decide to go walking in winter in either of the two above mentioned types of area, you would be well advised to go initially with someone more experienced than yourself. You will also need to think very carefully about the type of clothing and equipment taken.

Of greater interest to readers of this book will be the way in which winter conditions can affect less extreme forms of walking. Particularly on cold, wet and windy days, you run a risk from hypothermia if you are out in the open for any length of time without being adequately clothed (see Chapter 14). Although a moderately high rate of heat loss should not present a serious risk to a reasonably fit adult during a short stroll, it can be extremely serious to both the young and the elderly, especially if they are out for more than a couple of hours. You should therefore wrap up warmly and carry extra spare clothing. Mittens or gloves (the latter being less effective) and a warm, woollen hat should be regarded as essential. You will also find it advantageous to carry a vacuum flask of hot drink (soup is ideal) and extra high-energy snacks.

When reasonably firm and well consolidated, snow can be a superb surface on which to walk. However, it can occur in several other forms. It may, for example, be soft and unconsolidated, in which case walking through it will be extremely tiring and more akin to wading through treacle. In open terrain it may camouflage the path, making navigation more of a problem than when following the same route in summer. It may also blow across pools and small streams, the first you know about their presence being when you get a boot full of icy water. This is particularly dangerous if there is any ice around, for windblown snow can then cover small but deep pools, with obvious dangers.

Soft snow may be thinly crusted, the crust supporting your weight for two or three steps but then breaking, allowing you to sink, possibly up to your knees, destroying any attempt at a rhythm and possibly even causing injury. Beware, too, of hard-packed snow when there are slopes around; you do not have to be in the mountains for a slip to become dangerous. A friend of mine once tripped and rocketed down a long slope of hard-packed snow in the South Downs. The slide, he later said, was exhilarating; not so the injuries he received when he was finally stopped by a fence post at the base of the slope.

Ice, too, can cause a number of problems, most of which should be fairly obvious. However, apart from the ice that you can see and therefore avoid, in certain conditions it is possible for there to be a thin but almost invisible coating of ice on boulders and exposed rocks, and this will certainly cause problems if your route takes you across rocky terrain. Frozen turf can also be something of a hazard if very cold weather occurs shortly after rain, especially if there are steep slopes involved. On the positive side, sub-zero temperatures can effectively solidify muddy patches on paths, making it far easier to proceed than would otherwise be the case.

One final point worth considering is walking during a thaw. Apart from the fact that conditions underfoot are likely to be surprisingly wet, brushing against overhanging branches will often result in large dollops of wet snow falling down your neck. Further snow and ice conditions will be discussed in Chapter 13.

Camping

Although camping is often thought of as 'roughing it', the experience need not be an uncomfortable one. Assuming that you have adequate equipment for the type of conditions you are likely to meet (see Chapters 6–8), the most important considerations are those of choice of site and some form of camp routine.

Choice of site

Whether you are camping in an official site or 'rough camping', your campsite will need a number of features, the most important being shelter from the elements, particularly wind. This requires a little thought. For example, it would be foolish to pitch your tent in the shelter of a cliff if there is a danger of falling rocks. Similarly, siting a camp beneath trees in stormy conditions incurs a certain risk. Conditions can worsen with surprising speed, especially in elevated areas, and wind can change direction within a few hours. Even in sheltered positions, you would be wise to pitch your tent with its back facing the direction of the prevailing (or expected) wind.

Try to find an area of ground which is not only level, but also fairly smooth. Tussocks, pebbles, tree roots and so on can cause a surprising amount of discomfort at night. If the ground is particularly uneven, you could pad the underneath of the groundsheet with something, and if you cannot find a patch of level ground, try to arrange the tent in such a way that you can sleep with your head upslope.

A further major consideration should be proximity to some form of water supply. At the same time, bear in mind that lakeside sites tend to be cold and damp and, at certain times of the year, you are likely to be plagued by insects. Sites on the banks of mountain streams can seem idyllic at first glance, but such streams, although pleasantly musical during the day, can be noisy at night, especially if it starts to rain. Furthermore, inviting, flat, green areas next to such streams are often highly prone to flooding, and even if the water does not rise to any extent, the ground can quickly become a quagmire even after a few hours of drizzle.

Establishing a routine

Having some form of routine when you camp will undoubtedly go a long way towards making the experience less prone to discomfort. This is particularly true in wet weather, when movement in and out of the tent should be kept to a minimum. Although many people go camping to get away from such things, you will find that, after only a few trips, the routine becomes less of a chore and more of a natural sequence of events which you do almost unconsciously.

Try to arrive at your site with plenty of time in which to pitch camp. Assuming that the weather is not so inclement that you need to get under shelter immediately, a brew on arrival will do wonders for morale. While the water is heating, try to get the 'feel' of the site, and work out the best position for the tent. Pitching should be done carefully and methodically, no matter how good or bad the weather. Once the tent is up, lay out your sleeping bag and place all other items in positions where they are readily accessible when needed. If it is raining, try to remove wet clothing before entering the tent and, no matter what the weather, never wear boots inside. If any water does find its way into the inner tent, mop it up immediately, before it has a chance to spread.

Cooking should also be done carefully and methodically; the majority of camping injuries are burns and scalds. Avoid cooking in the tent unless it is impossible to do so outside, and take great care when refuelling the stove, adjusting the flame, stirring the contents of pans and so on. The quality of the food you produce can make or break a camping trip, for you will undoubtedly have a ravenous appetite by virtue of the energy expended during the day.

When striking camp in wet weather it may be wise to leave one tent standing until everything else has been cleared away; if this is done, you will, at least, be able to pack such things as sleeping bags and spare clothing in relatively dry conditions. If you are away for two or three days and only have one set of dry clothing, it is far better to keep this for use when in camp and to put on wet clothing at the start of each day – not a very comfortable experience, but better than having no dry clothing at all.

Finally, when everything is packed away and you are about to leave, cast your eyes carefully over the site to double check that nothing has been left behind, including litter. Within a day or so of you leaving, there should be nothing to indicate that anyone has camped in the area.

Load carrying

No matter how fit you are or how good your rucksack, the way in which you pack the load will have a considerable bearing both on the psychological weight (i.e. the weight you feel) and on the comfort of the journey. The following remarks are concerned mainly with backpacking rucksacks and, therefore, with heavier loads than are carried during the average day walk. However, the principles of load carrying remain the same no matter what the weight of the load or the size of the rucksack.

The most important thing to realise is that the load should be carried in such a way that the weight bears as directly as possible onto the pelvic girdle and hence onto the legs. Many older rucksacks, particularly those which are wider at the bottom than the top, throw the majority of the weight onto the shoulders and the spine, and although this is not much of a problem when carrying the type of light loads usually associated with low-level, summer strolls, the bent-forward posture which you need to adopt with this type of rucksack can lead to all sorts of problems during longer backpacking trips. Generally speaking, you would be wise to consider a well designed, modern rucksack as an essential requirement for all but the lightest of loads, the principle design features of which have already been discussed in Chapter 6.

When packing your rucksack, there are a number of things to take into consideration, not the least of which is the order in which you are going to need the various items. For example, it is little use packing your waterproofs right at the bottom of the sack if the weather forecast tells you it is likely to rain. You should also aim to achieve as well balanced a load as possible, preferably with the heavier items towards the top. The better balanced the ruck-sack, the less muscular energy will be needed to carry it, and the less likely you are to trip up, even though a heavy sack is bound to alter your centre of gravity to a certain degree. This difference in balance is something that should be borne in mind when crossing rough terrain or scrambling when carrying a heavy rucksack.

Hard items or objects with sharp corners and edges should be positioned well away from the outside of the rucksack, particularly where they may dig into your back. Additionally, it is better to avoid hanging objects such as water flasks from the outside of the rucksack as they tend to snag on any overhanging branches, swing around uncontrollably, and quickly become an annoyance both to you and your companions.

Although everyone has their own method of packing, and you, through trial and error, should choose the method which you find the most comfortable, it is worth noting that many experienced backpackers pack in a remarkably similar way. Their sleeping bag, possibly contained in a compression sack, normally goes at the bottom of the rucksack together, perhaps, with some spare clothing; their tent, cooking equipment and possibly some food usually goes towards the top, and items needed during the journey are either packed in side pockets, the top pouch pocket or at the very top. A first-aid kit will usually fit in a side pocket or the top pouch, and emergency food and a survival bag can be left permanently in the bottom of the rucksack. Some people roll their sleepmat tightly and strap it at the bottom or the top, others unroll it and use is as a waterproof liner, an added advantage being that it has a noticeable cushioning effect.

As well as packing to achieve a balanced load, you will also need to be fairly space-conscious for you will have a limited amount of room. Do not forget that things such as mugs and cooking pans may well contain a fair amount of wasted space which can often be filled with smaller items. Consider, too, that it may be preferable to repack certain foodstuffs in different containers from that in which they were bought; this is particularly true of items sold in glass containers, for not only is glass heavy and potentially dangerous, it is nowadays totally unnecessary. Whilst on the subject of foodstuffs, it is a wise precaution to pack food and fuel in totally separate areas. Indeed, liquid fuels, even when carried in the correct type of container, are best kept in side pockets where any leak will not be so potentially disastrous.

As has already been mentioned, no rucksack can be relied upon to be totally waterproof in all weather conditions, and you would be wise not only to use a rucksack liner of some description, but also to store particularly vulnerable items such as sleeping bags and spare clothing in plastic bags or waterproof stuff sacks.

Finally, the heavier the load you carry, the more energy you will be using, and the longer it will take you to travel any given distance. You should take such things into consideration not only when planning your routes (and booking your overnight accommodation or campsite), but also when planning your meals. All the energy you use will have to be supplied via food, and the quality of your menus will be particularly important on extended trips such as when backpacking along the longer long-distance footpaths.

11

Map
Interpretation

One of the most useful skills a walker can have is not only the ability to read a map, but also to interpret it. Interpreting the map means, almost literally, that you are able to visualise the landscape – relating what you see on the map to the landscape around you, and vice versa. Unfortunately, map interpretation is not something that can be learned from a book. It requires practical experience, and the more you practise, the easier it becomes. The most important thing to understand is that a good map is simply an accurate picture of the ground as seen from above, with relative size and distance indicated by drawing the map to a particular scale, and features represented by symbols known as conventional signs. These will be laid out in the key of whatever map you are using, divided into sections on roads and paths, general features, water features and so on.

One way of developing your map interpretation skills is, next time you go out in a car, to take a map of the area with you and try to trace your journey. Relate what you can see from the window to what you can see on the map – rivers, patches of woodland, built-up areas, churches and so on. Once you are happy with this, try to predict what you will see around the next bend, or over the brow of the next hill. If you can do this successfully when you are in a car, you should be able to do it even more successfully when you are out walking, when everything is happening at a slower pace! There should be no need for you to walk along, map in hand at all times. Indeed, if your map interpretation is good, you may only have to consult it on the odd occasion.

Scale

The scale of a map is simply the way in which it represents distance. Because scale is often referred to in terms of a ratio (e.g. 1:50,000), many people feel that it is complicated. In fact, the principle is very simple. If a map has a scale of 1:50,000, it simply means that one unit of length on the map is equal to 50,000 units of the same length on the ground. Thus, at this scale, 1 cm on the map represents 50,000 cm on the ground; 50,000 cm is equal to 500 m which is the same as half a kilometre. Thus, at a scale of 1:50,000, 1 cm is equal to half a kilometre.

A further area of confusion is the difference between large scale and small scale. Simply, large-scale maps show more detail than small-scale maps. Taking our 1:50,000 scale map as an example, it squeezes a ground distance of 1 km into a map distance of 2 cm, and the amount of detail that it can show is obviously limited by the amount of space available on the map. If, however, we had a map which was drawn at a scale of 1:25,000, where 1 km on the ground was represented by *4 cm* on the map – i.e. a *larger* scale – there would be twice as much space available, thus far more detail could be shown.

One aspect worth noting when travelling through particularly hilly terrain is that, because a map is flat, map distance is a measure of length over a flat surface. Thus map distance does not take into consideration the extra distances you have to walk when you wander up and down the slopes. Although this difference is usually negligible, you would be wise to bear it in mind not only when going for long walks in hilly areas, but also when doing any coastal walking where your route may take you from headland to head-land via the beach.

The two scales most commonly used by walkers are 1:50,000 and 1:25,000. Although 1:50,000 scale maps are usually adequate, 1:25,000 scale maps show considerably more detail, and are useful when visiting a new area, working out routes along less well trodden paths or travelling through mountainous or more remote moorland areas. Ideally, you should gain experience of using maps of both scales, and should be able to tell them apart at a glance. Although there are many noticeable differences, mainly in terms of the amount of detail shown, the easiest way to tell them apart initially is to look at the **grid lines**.

If you look at any Ordnance Survey map, you will see that it is divided into a series of squares by two sets of parallel lines, one set

running from top to bottom, the other, from side to side. These
lines are known as grid lines, the distance between them representing a distance of exactly one kilometre. The squares which
they form are known as **grid squares**, each representing an area
of one square kilometre. Thus, the lines will be 2 cm apart on
1:50,000 scale maps, and 4 cm apart on 1:25,000 scale maps.

Apart from giving you a quick reference as to distance, grid lines
have two further and very important uses. Firstly, they enable you
to measure accurate bearings (see Chapter 12); secondly, they can
be used to give the location of any feature, anywhere in the
country. This will obviously be useful if you wish to describe a
particular location, for whatever the reason. This is done by
working out what is known as a **grid reference**.

To give the approximate location of a feature, you can work out
a four-figure grid reference which locates the object to within an
area of one square kilometre. What you are doing, effectively, is
quoting the grid reference of the grid square in which the object is
situated. Defining this grid reference is very simple, the reference
consisting of a horizontal and vertical coordinate, as shown in
Figure 18. In the example given, the four-figure grid reference for
the church would be 2540.

Although there is only one square with the reference 2540 on
your map, there will be countless other squares with the same
reference all over the country. To be perfectly accurate you
should therefore also include the grid letters, and these will be
printed in the map's key (e.g. SO). The completed reference in this
instance would therefore be SO2540. It is obviously important
that you use the correct lines (i.e. *left of* then *below* the object),
in the right order. The final combination of letters and numbers is
unique, and can be used to work out the position of the feature on
any Ordnance Survey map, no matter what its scale.

It may sometimes be necessary to be a little more accurate, in
which case you can give a six-figure grid reference. In this, not
only do you give the reference of the grid square, you also locate
the feature within the square. Start in exactly the same way,
quoting the reference numbers of the grid line to the left of the
feature (e.g. 25). Now imagine that the distance between this line
and the one to the right is divided into tenths, and work out how
many tenths of a square the feature lies from the left-most line. If it
is five-tenths of the way across, the third figure of your grid
reference will be five (e.g. 255). If it is less than one-tenth away,
the third figure of our grid reference will be a zero. Now quote the

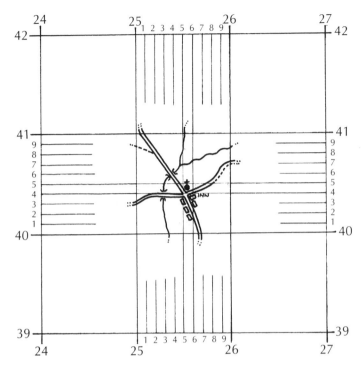

18. Calculating grid references. To calculate the grid reference of the church, find the reference number of the grid line immediately to its left (25). Estimate how many tenths of a square the church is to the right of this line (5). Now find the reference number of the grid line immediately below it (40). Estimate how many tenths of a square the church is above this line (4). The grid reference of the church is therefore 255404

reference numbers of the line below the feature (e.g. 40) and work out how many tenths of a square the feature lies above that line. If it is four-tenths up, the figure '4' will be the final figure of your grid reference (e.g. 404). The final six-figure grid reference in this instance will be 255404, and you can add the grid letters if necessary.

Don't worry if you forget all this in the field; an explanation of how to calculate a six-figure grid reference can be found in the key of any Ordnance Survey map. The beauty of this system is that it is virtually open ended. If you want to give a more precise location, you can quote an eight-figure reference. This is calculated in exactly the same way except that, instead of working out the tenths, you work out the hundredths. Obviously this is difficult to do with any accuracy on a 1:50,000 scale map, but it is perfectly feasible when using scales of 1:25,000 and larger.

Conventional signs

Initially, you may find it tiresome having constantly to refer to the key to find out what a particular symbol means, but many are self-explanatory and, in any case, you will soon learn the more common ones.

A common, early mistake is to confuse the symbol for a boundary and the symbol for a footpath. Many people have spent hours looking for a non-existent footpath, becoming more and more convinced that they are lost, when all the time they are crossing and recrossing a boundary.

It may be useful to think of conventional signs in terms of four categories. The first consists of all those signs which have no representation on the ground and which therefore are of little use when trying to pinpoint your position. These will include a whole host of boundaries (but not field boundaries – see page 109), sites of battles and other antiquities, and spot heights. It also includes the symbols for the various public rights of way.

If you look at your map carefully, you will see that there are separate symbols for rights of way and for footpaths. A right of way is purely a line along which one may legally travel – just because it is shown on your map does not necessarily mean that one can find any indication of its existence on the ground. A footpath, on the other hand, will generally be noticeable on the ground, but just because it is there does not mean that one has any right to walk along it. The symbols for both are often printed one on top of the other. Where this happens, one can generally expect to find a path along which one may legally walk. There are exceptions, however, as we will see later.

Second are the 'area' signs which give details of the type of terrain. Included in this category are the symbols for bouldery ground, rough grazing, types of woodland and marsh. Unless such areas occur in small, isolated patches, they are of limited use when trying to pinpoint position, although they can give a rough idea of where one is and can be very useful when planning a walk.

The third category of conventional signs includes all those which represent linear features such as roads, railways, rivers, canals, electricity transmission lines and footpaths. Long field boundaries and the edges of forestry plantations can also be regarded in the same way. Although, when taken in isolation, such features cannot be used to pinpoint position, they can give you an approximate location and can be used. as 'handrails' which can lead one to a definite spot. Where two linear features meet or cross, such as at road or river junctions, this combination can be used to pinpoint position.

Finally, we have those conventional signs which indicate 'point' features and which can therefore be used by themselves to pinpoint position. This category includes such things as churches, isolated buildings, bridges and 'trig. points'. A trig. point (or triangulation station) is a concrete pillar which is used for surveying purposes by the Ordnance Survey, usually located at or near the summit of a hill.

It is, of course, far easier to work out your position when you are standing beside a definite feature than when standing in the middle of nowhere. If there are no convenient, single 'point' features, you may be able to use a combination of things such as a stream leaving a patch of woodland. You should think about such combinations very carefully, and keep your eyes open for suitable combinations as you walk along. As has already been mentioned, successful navigation is very much a matter of observation, both in terms of what is shown on the map and what you can see on the ground.

It is important that you make no assumptions when interpreting the various conventional signs. A good example is shown by the symbol for field boundaries which can be found on 1:25,000 scale maps. Many people make the mistake of thinking that this symbol always shows stone walls whereas, in fact, the boundary could be anything from a fence or a hedge to a ditch or a bank of earth.

You should also bear in mind that a map is out of date as soon as it is printed, since it is static, whereas the landscape is dynamic. Roads can be improved, valleys can be dammed to form reservoirs, new housing estates can spring up and modern forestry often uses trees which mature in a remarkably short space of time. It is not impossible that, since the completion of the survey upon which your map is based, a new forest has been planted and has grown to maturity. Conversely, a mature plantation may have been felled and the ground cleared. Alternatively, a path which was reasonably well defined when the survey was done may have fallen into disuse and have become overgrown, there now being little, if any, sign of it on the ground.

In the British Isles the one thing which will stay reasonably constant is the 'shape' of the land. We are lucky enough not to suffer from major earthquakes or volcanic activity, so the topography of the landscape remains remarkably constant. Where this is not the case, such as, for example, in quarrying, the changes will be very obvious. Bearing this in mind, there is one conventional sign which is extremely important: the contour line. An understanding of both contour lines and the patterns made by them is essential to map interpretation.

Contours

The way in which map makers represent the shape of the land, the hills and the valleys is by using a conventional sign known as a contour line. This is simply an imaginary line joining points of equal height, with the difference in height between all the points on one contour and all the points on the next known as the 'vertical interval'. (This is specified in the map key.) If the vertical interval is, say, 5 m, you can tell that all the points touched by any one particular contour line are 5 m higher than points touched by the contour line below it, and 5 m lower than points on the contour line above it.

In order to visualise how contour lines represent the shape of the land, it may be helpful to imagine a pyramid built of bricks. Looking at one of its faces sideways on, you would see a line of mortar in between each of the courses of bricks. These lines of mortar can be thought of as contour lines, the vertical interval being the difference in height between one line of mortar and the next.

If you were now to look at the pyramid from directly above, you would see that the lines of mortar form a series of squares, one inside the other. If you know the size of the pyramid (i.e. the scale) and the thickness of the bricks (i.e. the vertical interval), it is a fairly simple job to work out its shape from this pattern of lines.

A similar thing can be done on a map. You know the scale, the key will tell you the vertical interval between the contour lines, so you can work out the shape of the landscape by looking at the patterns formed by the contour lines.

Because the shape of the land is infinitely variable, working out the patterns can sometimes appear to be quite complicated, certainly at first glance. Luckily, there are a few 'rules' which will

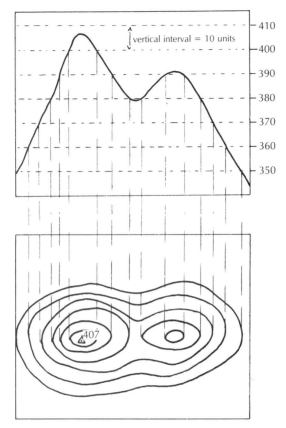

19. *Working out the shape of the landscape from the contour lines. In this example the feature is a twin peak.*

help. Firstly, the closer the contour lines are together, the steeper will be the slope. If there are five contour lines for a horizontal distance of 500 m, and a vertical interval of 10 m, you know that the land rises by 50 m over that distance. If, however, there are ten contour lines, the land must rise by 100 m, and the slope must therefore be steeper. Secondly, there are only a few basic patterns which you need to know in order to be able to work out the shape of the landscape. For example, a pattern in the shape of a 'V' can show both a valley and a spur, and although a series of parallel lines will always show a smooth slope, you will not initially be able to tell which way the slope faces. In order to be able to identify a shape from a pattern, you need to be able to work out the 'aspect

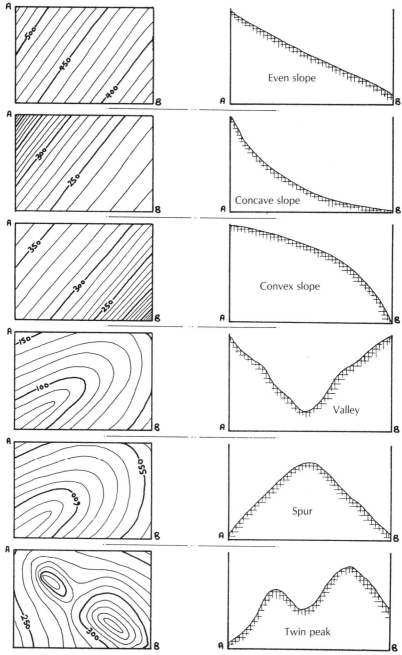

20. *Examples of contour patterns and the features they represent*

of slope' – which is up and which is down. There are a number of ways in which this can be done.

Firstly, where space permits, some of the contour lines will be overprinted with the height that they represent. If one line represents, say, 200 m, and another, 300 m, one can tell at a glance the aspect of slope. However, only one contour need be printed with its height, because the figures are always printed facing uphill (i.e. the top of the figure points to the top of the slope).

Secondly, one can look at other conventional signs in the area. There may be a trig. point nearby, invariably situated at or near a high point. Similarly, there may be one or more 'spot heights' (heights of individual points) shown, and whilst these are purely map symbols, and do not have any representative feature on the ground, they can be extremely useful when trying to work out the aspect of slope.

Local drainage, too, can be used to great effect. If, for example, there is a 'V' pattern of contour lines with a river flowing along the middle, it is most likely a valley (rivers rarely flow along the tops of spurs!) Although in hilly areas it is usually possible to work out the aspect of slope fairly quickly, in flatter terrain it may be necessary to trace a river either to its source or a confluence, by which time a couple of spot heights may have been passed. Examples of some of the more common patterns and the shapes they represent are shown in Figure 20.

Although it will generally be sufficient to work out the rough shape of the land, it is possible to be extremely detailed if the situation demands it. Instead of seeing simply a slope, you should be able to work out whether the slope is concave or convex, or whether it is regular or stepped. Indeed, every little squiggle on a contour line represents some facet of the shape of the land, and, with practice, each can be identified.

12

Using a Compass

Although map interpretation is central to successful navigation, and in itself will be sufficient when using well defined footpaths, a few additional techniques will also be found useful. The most obvious of these involves the use of a compass.

Modern compasses come in a wide variety of shapes and sizes; however, there is really only one choice for walking purposes, this being a 'protractor' or 'orienting' compass, often known as a 'Silva' compass. Although Silva was for many years a brand leader, good orienting compasses are now available from a number of other firms, Suunto and Recta being but two.

Referring to Figure 21, which shows a typical compass of this type, you will see that it can be thought of as consisting of two separate parts: the compass housing (1), and the base plate (2). **The compass housing** comprises a sealed, circular plastic capsule which is filled with a clear oil, and which contains a *magnetic needle* (3), one half of which is red, the other half being white. The red end is known as the north-seeking end because, when used correctly, it will point directly towards a point on the earth's surface known as magnetic north. Around the top rim of the housing are a number of divisions, each one representing 2° of arc. Some of these divisions are numbered, and the relative positions of the cardinal points (i.e. north, south, east and west) are also shown. The base of the housing is engraved with a number of fine, parallel lines known as *orienting lines* (4), the central ones being joined together to form the *orienting arrow* (5). The point of this arrow corresponds exactly to the position of north as marked on the top rim.

The **base plate**, also made of clear plastic, should ideally be at least 10 cm long. Although it is possible to buy compact orienting compasses with shorter base plates, you may have difficulty if you use these to calculate bearings on 1:25,000 scale maps, and I would recommend that you choose a model with a larger base plate unless you intend to walk only on well trodden footpaths using 1:50,000 scale maps. Whatever the size of the base plate, it should be engraved with three or more fine lines running parallel to the sides, the central one of which intersects the compass housing (6). It is at this point that you read your bearings. At the far end of this central line there will also be a large arrow pointing away from the compass housing. This is known as the *direction-of-travel arrow* (7).

In addition to all these features, there will usually be some form of *magnifying lens* (8) which may help when interpreting small features, and one or more *scales* (9), the most useful being printed in centimetres. These scales can be used both to measure distances on the map and to calculate grid references accurately.

Some of the more expensive compasses, particularly those with larger base plates, will have a further set of scales known as Romer scales. In these, the conversion from map distance to ground

(1) Compass housing
(2) Base plate
(3) Compass needle
(4) Orienting lines
(5) Orienting arrow
(6) Point at which bearings are read
(7) Direction-of-travel arrow
(8) Magnifying lens
(9) Scales

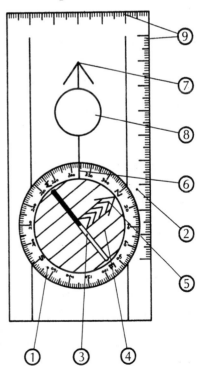

21. The orienting compass

distance has already been calculated, enabling you to read off a distance without having to juggle millimetres into metres. The standard conversions used on Romer scales are equivalent to the maps most commonly used (i.e. 1:25,000, 1:50,000 and 1:63,360 – the old inch-to-the-mile maps).

It is possible to buy most models of compasses in either luminous or non-luminous versions. The luminous versions are useful if you intend to do any night navigation, although they are not essential. If you do buy a luminous compass, make sure that there are luminous points on the direction-of-travel arrow, the orienting arrow, and the north-seeking end of the needle, and a fairly large luminous patch on the top rim of the housing where you read off the bearing.

One thing worth checking is the way in which the compass housing is attached to the base plate. Particularly on those models where the housing is removable, the method of attachment must be both secure and precise, fixing the line on the rim of the housing where you read off the bearings exactly in line with the end of the line containing the direction-of-travel arrow. Any movement here will lead to inaccuracies. Additionally, check that the housing is contained in some form of collar which enables it to be turned fairly easily through 360°. The quality of this movement varies quite considerably and is worth checking. Although there should be some resistance, it should be possible to turn the housing smoothly. If the resistance is too great, it will be difficult to set accurate bearings; if it is too weak, you run the risk that the housing will move accidentally, thereby altering any bearing which you may have set.

In addition to this type of orienting compass, there is one other version which you may come across. This is the sighting compass, and it comes in two forms: the optical sighting compass, and the mirror compass (see Figure 22). Of the two, the optical sighting compass is the easier to use. In essence, it is exactly the same as that described above, except it has two additional and very useful features: an optical prism inside a specially extended compass-housing capsule, and a 'ring' type needle which is divided into numbered segments. By looking through a small window in the side of the extended housing, you can sight onto objects and read off the bearing from the ring needle. Although this arrangement makes it possible to be far more accurate when following bearings, there are two major disadvantages. Firstly, due to the complexity of the needle, it is sometimes awkward to measure bearings on the map (see next section). Secondly, it is far more expensive.

22. Sighting compasses. An optical sighting compass (left) and mirror compass (right). Note the small base plate on the mirror compass

Although many people swear by mirror sighting compasses, they suffer from the same disadvantages of high cost and complex needle. They also tend to have small base plates, and many people find the mirror arrangement a little confusing. If you decide that you need the type of accuracy which can be gained by sighting compasses, and can justify the cost, I have no hesitation in recommending that you buy one of the optical sighting models.

Navigating with a compass

Apart from its use as a magnifying lens (to aid the interpretation of complex parts of the map) and for its scales (Romer or otherwise) to measure distances and to work out accurate grid references, the main use of the orienting compass is for the measurement of bearings. When used correctly, it allows not only the measurement of accurate bearings both from the map and from the ground, but also enables one to follow this bearing with great accuracy once the necessary calculation has been done.

I must emphasise, yet again, that the most important part of successful walking navigation lies in the use of the map. No matter how good your compass technique, it is useless unless you have at least a modicum of skill at map interpretation. In all but the most difficult terrain or the worst of conditions, you should be able to find your way around using the map alone, especially if you are following a footpath.

First and foremost, you must have some knowledge about the points of the compass in relation to your map. All Ordnance Survey maps are drawn with their tops pointing towards the north. The grid lines running up and down the map point towards north (at the top) and south (at the bottom). The grid lines running across the map therefore point west (to the left) and east (to the right).

One useful technique is that of 'setting' the map. In most situations you should be able to do this without using a compass. It is easiest to do when you can refer to an obvious linear feature such as a road or a river, or even the path along which you are walking. All you do is turn the map so that the linear feature on the map runs in exactly the same direction as you see it running on the ground. If this is done correctly, everything to your left on the ground will also appear to the left of your position on the map. If, for example, you are walking in a southerly direction, your correctly set map will be upside down.

It is also possible to set your map using your compass. This is a useful technique for those occasions when there are few linear features, or when visibility is poor. Put your compass on the map so that the direction-of-travel arrow points towards the top, and the sides of the base plate run parallel to the sides of the map. Turn the compass housing so that the orienting arrow also points to the top of the map and is exactly in line with the direction-of-travel arrow. The indicated bearing should read N. Now, keeping the compass firmly in this position, turn the map and compass together until the red end of the compass needle lies directly over the orienting arrow, as shown in Figure 23. When this is done, your map will be set to within a few degrees. As it happens, there will be a slight error when using the compass in this way, for you have not allowed for something called magnetic variation (see page 122). However, this error is so small that it will almost invariably be unimportant when using the compass to set the map.

Another useful technique is that of using the compass to get a rough idea of the direction in which you are travelling. Hold the compass in front of you with the direction-of-travel arrow pointing in the direction in which you are travelling. Now turn the compass

Top of map

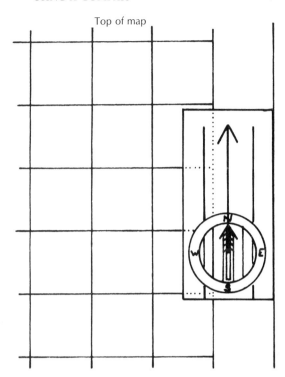

23. Setting the map
with a compass

housing until the orienting arrow lies directly underneath the red
end of the needle. The bearing indicated where the line from the
direction-of-travel arrow intersects the compass housing will be
the direction in which you are travelling. Here again, this will not
be exactly correct because of magnetic variation, but the amount
of error will be so small as to be virtually insignificant in the vast
majority of cases.

A third technique, again not precise, but extremely useful
nonetheless, is that of being able to locate yourself on a linear
feature. Whilst this feature will usually be something like a path or
a road, the same technique could be used when, for example, you
are walking along a ridge or the top of a long slope. What you need
is some point feature which you can identify both on the ground
and on the map. If you can identify such a feature, hold the
compass in front of you so that the direction-of-travel arrow is
pointing directly at this feature, then turn the compass housing so
that the orienting arrow lies directly underneath the red end of
the needle. Once done, put the compass on the map in such a way
that one side of the base plate lies against the feature on which you

have just sighted then, without turning the compass housing and keeping the edge of the base plate firmly against the feature, turn the whole of the compass until the orienting lines are parallel to the north–south grid lines, and the orienting arrow points towards the top of the map. You can ignore the compass needle. If you have done this correctly, the side of the base plate which lies against the feature will also cut across the linear feature on which you are standing, and the point at which they intersect will be your approximate position (see Figure 24).

These techniques are obviously of great help when you are following a definite feature (e.g. a path or a ridge, etc.) in conditions of reasonable visibility. However, particularly if you walk in open country such as can be found in mountain and moorland

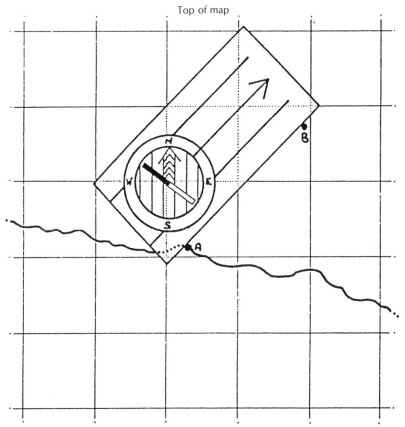

24. Location on a linear feature

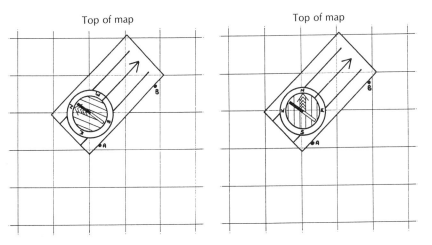

25. *Calculating a bearing (1)*   26. *Calculating a bearing (2)*

areas, you may well need to be far more precise. It is in situations such as this that it may be necessary for you to calculate and then walk along a specific bearing. An orienting compass makes this easy.

A **bearing** is quite simply the angle between two imaginary lines. For our purposes, one of these lines will be that running between our present position and north, the other will be that running between our present position and the point to which we wish to go. Let us assume that you are standing at an identifiable position on a map. We will call this position point A. You wish to go to another identifiable position, point B. Place your compass on the map in such a way that the direction-of-travel arrow points towards point B, and one side of the base plate forms a line between the two points (see Figure 25). Be as accurate as you can – the side of the base plate must touch both points. Now, *without moving the base plate*, turn the compass housing so that the orienting arrow points towards the top (northern) edge of the map, and the orienting lines are exactly parallel to the north–south grid lines. Again, be precise. It will help if you move the compass so that you can get one of the orienting lines to lie directly over one of the north–south grid lines (see Figure 26). You have now measured the bearing, the value being shown at the position where the line from the direction-of-travel arrow intersects the top rim of the compass housing.

So far you have used your compass purely as a protractor with which to measure the bearing. You are now going to use it to follow this bearing. Hold the compass in front of you with the direction-of-travel arrow pointing away from you. *Without moving the compass housing*, turn round until the north-seeking end of the needle lies directly over the orienting arrow. The direction-of-travel arrow will now be pointing towards point B – well, almost!

There is one small problem: there is more than one north! When measuring the bearing from the map, you measured the angle between a line from point A to point B, and a line from point A to grid north – the north to which the grid lines point. This bearing is therefore known as a **grid bearing**. Unfortunately, the needle on your compass points to a different position: magnetic north. The difference between these two norths is known as the **magnetic variation**, and although it is only a matter of a few degrees, you must adjust your bearing if you wish to be at all accurate. A grid bearing which has been adjusted to take account of magnetic variation is known as a **magnetic bearing**.

The magnetic variation is not a constant figure, but alters both from year to year and from map to map. Its value will always be printed somewhere in the key of your map. You will also see a reference to a point called true north. (This can be ignored for our purposes). In this country, magnetic north is slightly to the west of grid north, and although it is reducing slightly every year, it will remain to the west for some time to come. This means you add the amount of the variation to the grid bearing (see Figure 27). Once you understand the principle of magnetic variation, you will begin to see that you can use it to be far more accurate whenever you use your compass.

Once you have calculated your magnetic bearing and have adjusted your compass accordingly, when you line up the north-seeking end of the needle with the orienting arrow, the direction-of-travel arrow will point exactly towards point B.

Following this bearing is simplicity itself. What you do is hold the compass up slightly, line up the north-seeking end of the needle with the orienting arrow, then sight along the line of the direction-of-travel arrow until you find a readily identifiable object that lies directly on your course. Once done, you can dispense with the compass and walk to that object. You then sight along the compass again, and so on, until you reach your destination. The

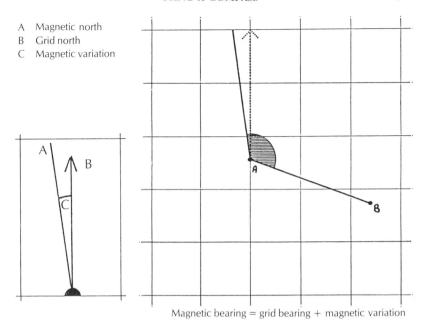

A   Magnetic north
B   Grid north
C   Magnetic variation

Magnetic bearing = grid bearing + magnetic variation

27. Magnetic variation

delight of using this system is that you do not have to walk precisely in a straight line. If, for example, there is a pool in the way, you can walk round it. So long as you eventually reach the object which you have chosen, it does not really matter what route you choose to get there.

By using your compass in the ways described, you can be remarkably accurate when walking through the most featureless of terrain. However, always bear in mind that your compass needle is magnetic. If you try to use magnetic bearings when standing near metal objects, these will affect the direction in which the needle points, thereby causing an error. You should therefore never use a magnetic bearing when standing, for example, by a metal gate, or under electricity transmission cables. Additionally, some camera exposure meters contain fairly powerful magnets, and these, too, can affect the accuracy of your compass. So long as you are aware of such things and are careful of the positions from which you read magnetic bearings, you should not go far wrong.

Other techniques

On most occasions it is possible to navigate by means of the skills and techniques mentioned in the previous sections. However, there may be times, such as when walking in mountainous areas or crossing remote moorlands, when a few additional techniques will be found useful.

In a previous section it was mentioned how the scale on your compass base plate can be used to measure distances fairly accurately. Knowing the distance between two points is one thing; being able to estimate that distance on the ground is a different matter. Although you may be able to judge when you have walked, say, 500 m along a road or a good path, your sense of distance may well forsake you when travelling across more rugged terrain. A useful piece of information to have at your fingertips, therefore, is the approximate number of paces you take to walk 100 m. The easiest way to find this out is to visit a local leisure centre (or some such similar place) where there is a 100 m running track marked out. Using your normal stride, walk the distance and count the number of times your left foot touches the ground (this is far easier than counting every single step). Do this three or four times, and work out the average number of double paces you take per hundred metres. This figure can then be put to good use when you are out walking.

You should realise, however, that your length of stride will alter according to the terrain and the angle of slope. On rough ground, or when ascending steep slopes, you will take more paces per hundred metres than when walking along a well laid path. Similarly, when walking down a smooth and easy slope, you may well take fewer paces. So long as you take these differences in the length of your stride into consideration, it is possible, with practice, to estimate distances extremely accurately using this technique.

Another useful technique is the ability to estimate how long it will take you to walk from one point to another. This can be done by using a formula known as **Naismith's Rule**. This states that you walk 5 km per hour, and that it will take an additional 30 minutes for every 300 m you climb. A rather unwieldy formula, perhaps, but by breaking it down it can become very useful. Instead of 5 km per hour, use 1 km in 12 minutes or even 500 m in 6 minutes. Instead of 30 minutes for every 300 m of ascent, use 10 minutes for every 100 m of ascent, or even 1 minute for every 10 m of ascent. Indeed, because the vertical interval of the contour lines on many maps is 10 m, you can work out the distance, work out the time for that distance, then add 1 minute for every contour line you cross when walking uphill.

Here again, your speed will depend on a number of factors, especially the conditions underfoot. Long climbs may well slow you down, as may long, steep descents. You will also travel more slowly if you are carrying a heavy rucksack or if the weather conditions are particularly bad. Despite this, like pacing, it is possible (with practice) to estimate time with a surprising degree of accuracy.

In particularly featureless terrain, there are a number of things you can do to help your compass technique. In some areas, for example, it may be difficult to find objects on which to sight when following a bearing. In this situation you can use another person as the object! Send a companion off in front of you, then sight along the compass in the normal way, getting your companion to move to the left or right until they are standing directly on course. You then walk to them, and repeat the exercise until either you reach your objective, or you can see an object which lies in the right position. If both of you have compasses, you can walk past your companion, and then he sights on you, and so on. This technique is known as **leap frogging**, and can be extremely useful in misty conditions.

Another technique, known as **aiming off**, can be used when you are heading towards a point on a linear feature. For the purposes of illustration, let us assume that you are heading across open terrain towards the junction of two paths, one of which lies across your course, the other being at a tangent. It is the path which goes off at a tangent that you wish to follow. You set a compass course and follow it, eventually reaching the path which lies across your course but, because of a slight error, not at the junction. You now have no idea in which direction the junction lies and if, like me, your life tends to be ruled by Murphy's law, you will inevitably head off in the wrong direction! If, however, you deliberately set your compass bearing to take you to one side of the junction, you should know in which direction to head when you reach the path (assuming, of course, you have not made a vast error). What, in fact, you are doing, is using the path which lies across your course as a 'handrail' which then leads you to the point for which you are trying to make.

With a degree of observance you should always know roughly

where you are, certainly to within, say, 1 km. This means that you should never be totally lost. Relocating yourself will be made that much easier if you are standing by a definite feature. You may, for example, be standing at a path junction, but your map shows that there are a number of path junctions in the area, and you are not quite sure which one is which. By using map interpretation, possibly in conjunction with one or more bearings, it should be relatively easy to work out your position. It is really simply a process of elimination.

There are several other useful techniques which can be applied to specific situations, but which are beyond the scope of this book. If you intend to visit more remote areas with any degree of regularity, you will undoubtedly find it useful to read a slightly more specialised book such as *Mountain Navigation Techniques* which deals with map interpretation and various additional skills in greater detail. Details of this and other titles will be found in Appendix IV.

PART V

Safety Factors

13

Weather

In Britain weather conditions make a marked contribution to walking. This does not mean, of course, that the activity need be restricted to warm, balmy days; some of my most memorable walks have been done in weather conditions which most people would have considered far from perfect: along the banks of a mountain stream in torrential rain, when the stream was in spate and the waterfalls were deafening; across the top of a rocky plateau in sub-zero temperatures when all the boulders were covered with huge flakes of hoar frost. Not only can different weather conditions enhance certain aspects of the environment through which you walk, they can also bring a number of problems, some very obvious, others less so.

Whatever the type of walking you intend to do, you should have a good idea of what to expect from the weather before you go. At one end of the spectrum, when, for example, going for a short afternoon stroll, it will often be sufficient simply to have listened to the weather forecast on the radio, or to have watched the television forecast the previous evening. Indeed, if you enjoy walking and intend to walk regularly, you should get into the habit of listening to television or radio weather forecasts on the off-chance that you will suddenly decide to go for a stroll the next day.

At the other end of the spectrum, when, for example, going into the mountains for a day or setting off on a backpacking trip, you should not only get as detailed a weather forecast as possible, but you should also make sure that the forecast is specifically for the area in which you intend to walk. Mountains, in particular, tend to make their own weather, and a national forecast – although giving you an idea of likely trends – will often be of little use in detail.

Area forecasts are available from a variety of sources such as local meteorological offices and some local radio stations. There may also be a recorded forecast available by telephone, details of which will be found in the directory. In many of the more popular walking areas, it may also be possible to get a forecast from a local information centre or even from a local specialist equipment shop.

It is one thing knowing what the weather is likely to do, but knowing how the expected conditions will affect your walking is another matter. The thing to realise is that weather conditions will affect you both directly and indirectly. For example, freezing temperatures will affect you directly by making you cold; they could also affect you indirectly by making the ground icy. Similarly, rain will affect you directly by making you wet; it will also affect you indirectly by making the ground wet, possibly making it slippery, raising stream levels, and causing a reduction in visibility. Generally speaking, the higher you go, the more severe will be the weather, and what seems like light drizzle carried on a breeze at sea level can be a raging storm with gale force winds and driving rain (or sleet) if you climb into the mountains.

One particular set of conditions which occurs with monotonous regularity in Britain is that of wind combined with rain. This combination can be particularly hazardous to the poorly clothed walker because of the effect known as **wind chill**. In still air, the human body loses a certain amount of heat through radiation, but if the air moves, the heat loss will be greater because fresh, cold air is constantly moving against the warm surface of the body, almost literally removing the heat as it passes. This is why some form of windproof clothing is so important. If, however, it is also raining and clothing becomes saturated, there is an additional heat loss via evaporation. This is why it is also important to carry some form of waterproof shell. Without these windproof and waterproof layers, you are at the mercy of the weather. Even in relatively low wind speeds, the amount of heat loss from a poorly protected body can be phenomenal and can lead, very rapidly, to the onset of hypothermia, a potentially fatal condition (see Chapter 14).

Poor visibility

Poor visibility is often associated with low cloud, hill fog and mist. However, there are several other ways in which visibility can be affected.

28. Walking in misty conditions. Even when following a well-defined path you will need to concentrate on your navigation when walking in conditions of poor visibility

All types of cloud, including mist and fog, are composed of minute droplets of water which slowly sink through the air. In addition to the fact that these airborne droplets effectively reduce the distance which you can see, they can also make you surprisingly wet. If, furthermore, there is movement of air, such as could be found when walking through low cloud on a windy moor, the need for waterproofs increases, if only to reduce the amount of heat loss caused by evaporation.

Misty conditions create their own beauty, making the landscape seem bigger and more mysterious, with all the normal reference points hidden. One of the most noticeable effects is that it becomes difficult to judge distances, hence the importance of good navigation. In very poor visibility, you will often find the skills of pacing and timing extremely useful.

In addition to mist and fog, rain can effectively blot out large portions of the landscape and, particularly when heavy or prolonged, may even cause you to hunch down into your waterproof shell, your world being reduced to a hood-bordered patch around your splashing feet.

Hail, too, can have a similar effect, especially when carried on a driving, turbulent wind. I have known walkers who have had their faces cut by wind-driven hail, and trying to peer into even a mild hailstorm can be a painful experience. When caught in such conditions, it is usually better to find shelter and sit it out, rather than press on regardless, for hailstorms rarely last for any length of time.

One of the worst conditions which you can meet is that of blizzard, which can effectively reduce your visibility to less than a couple of metres. Indeed, in a true blizzard you will find it difficult to move at all, and you could literally be standing on the edge of a precipice without even realising that it was there! If the weather forecast suggests a combination of winds and snowfall, you would be well advised to stay away from the hills and any large open areas. Although true 'white out' conditions are rare south of the Scottish borders, they can occur in any of the British mountain areas, and I have even known them to occur on the South Downs.

A blizzard is simply a combination of high winds and snowfall, with each component having a part to play. Even on calm days, falling snow has a considerable effect on visibility, and can cause several other problems (see next section). Wind, too, can reduce the amount that you can see, particularly if you are walking straight into it, and the dry, dusty winds of summer can be as bad as the icy blasts of winter, both bringing tears to the eyes.

Last but by no means least, do not underestimate the problems which darkness can bring. Particularly when walking in the hills in winter, days can be surprisingly short and dusk can change into the depths of night with dismaying rapidity. Although there is little to beat walking across open countryside on a frosty night, the sky alive with pin-sharp stars or the landscape bright with moonlight, you will more commonly be faced with a dim, often dismal darkness in which you stumble and trip at every step. Planning to walk at night is one thing; being caught out unexpectedly is a totally different proposition. Even if you carry a torch you will probably find the going fairly tough and the navigation fraught with potential difficulties.

Snow and ice

Walking through countryside which is clad in snow and ice can be a fantastic experience. Everything seems bigger and more remote, and you can get a tremendous feeling of adventure from what, in summer, would have been the most straightforward of journeys. However, despite the exhilaration, there can also be several pitfalls.

In addition to the reduction in visibility caused by falling snow, there are further problems once the snow has settled. If, for example, the temperature is particularly cold and the snow is relatively fresh, the flakes will not bind together and any wind will pick up the individual crystals, not only causing drifting, but also effectively reducing the visibility as much, if not more, than when it was falling. This can also lead to weird effects such as when the layer of moving snow is only a few centimetres thick, hiding the ground from your knees down in a swirling mass of ice crystals, but leaving the rest of the landscape almost perfectly clear.

When the snow has finally settled several other problems are possible, not the least of which is that drifts can effectively camouflage objects and features which are usually highly visible. Not only can this pose problems so far as map interpretation is concerned (you can, after all, only interpret that which you can see), it can also cause potential hazards by concealing, for example, a narrow but deep ditch, or ice on a deep, frozen pool.

Most of the effects of ice should be fairly obvious. Extra care should be taken in conditions where there is ice on rocks, when going along the banks of rushing rivers or along the tops of steep slopes and cliffs. During a thaw, do not forget to look up before passing under cliffs and outcrops of rock – there may be large lumps of ice or sharp, pointed icicles held in place by a tenuous anchorage which is rapidly melting. Falls of rock are also much more likely during thaw conditions. Ice forming in cracks on cliffs will prise away rocks from the slope where they will be held in place until a thaw. When the ice melts, gravity takes over and the rock falls.

It is, of course, in the mountains that the effects of snow and ice are most noticeable. Avalanches, for example, are a far more common danger than many people think, and even where there is no immediate danger from avalanche, ground conditions can present a range of difficulties. The snow may be so compacted by the wind that walking on it is like walking on ice. In such conditions, a simple slip may turn into an uncontrollable slide – the consequences of which do not bear thinking about if you happen to be in craggy territory. On the other hand, the snow may be deep and soft, in which case forward momentum will only be possible with enormous effort.

14

Medical Matters

Hypothermia

Hypothermia or, perhaps more correctly in our context, exhaustion-exposure is, unquestionably, the most insidious condition that you will ever meet whilst walking. Although of most concern to mountain and moorland walkers, given the right conditions it can occur almost anywhere, even on the Cheshire Plains, and certainly on some of the long-distance coastal paths.

There are a number of problems. Firstly, hypothermia may be difficult to diagnose, particularly in its early stages, and can creep up on you unawares; at other times it can be sudden and catastrophic. In both cases it is vital that it be treated as early as possible as it can be less than two hours between onset and death. Not only may the sufferer start behaving irrationally, resisting, both abusively and sometimes violently, all your efforts to help him, he may, paradoxically, think he is too hot and start taking off his clothes.

In order to understand how to treat exhaustion-exposure, you need to know a little about its cause and effects.

The body can be considered in two parts: the 'core', containing all the vital organs, and the 'shell' – the flesh and bones which surround the core. Of the two, the core is the more important because it is this which keeps us alive. To work efficiently, the vital organs must be kept at a constant temperature, which, in the human body, is 37°C. If this temperature rises or falls by even a small amount, the organs will begin to lose their efficiency and may malfunction. The greater the rise and fall in temperature, the greater the severity of the malfunction.

The body normally maintains this temperature to within a very fine range, balancing out heat losses and gains via a number of mechanisms. Heat is gained through such things as stored energy, muscular activity, taking a hot bath, eating hot food and so on; and is lost into the surrounding air by, for instance, sweating. In this process the body allows moisture to pass to the surface of the skin where it can evaporate, taking heat with it. The reason you feel flushed at the same time is because all the capillaries (tiny blood vessels) which lie just beneath the skin have dilated (opened up) to allow more warm blood to flow close to the skin where it can shed its heat.

One of the immediate physical effects of being too cold is shivering, in which the body causes muscles to go into spasm in order to create more heat. The reason you fumble when you shiver is not only because of the muscular activity, but also because some of the surface capillaries have constricted (closed down), reducing the amount of warm blood which flows near the skin and thus decreasing the heat loss still further. This closing of the capillaries is known as *vaso-constriction*.

When you go out walking, particularly in wet and windy conditions, you are entering an environment in which the body can lose heat faster than it can be produced. This is why being properly clothed is so important. The overall heat loss can be made worse if, for example, you are undertaking a particularly strenuous walk and have not eaten sufficient energy-giving food, for your body will simply not be able to produce enough heat to balance out the excessive heat loss. The end result will be hypothermia – a reduction in the temperature of the core.

So what happens as the heat loss continues? Although there are a number of phases which can be identified, everyone is affected in a slightly different way. Signs and symptoms of the various phases may overlap or may even be absent, so the following is purely a guide to what you *may* see.

As mentioned above, the initial affect will be shivering and constriction of the surface capillaries. If the temperature of the core continues to drop, the shivering may increase in intensity, possibly accompanied by cramp, eventually becoming uncontrollable.

At a core temperature of around 35°C, the vaso-constriction will be so marked that the blood supply to some of the muscles in the limbs will be reduced and this will cause the victim to stumble and display a general lack of co-ordination. The brain, too, will start to become affected, and the victim may become withdrawn and lethargic.

Up to this point, the condition can be described as *mild hypothermia*, although one should not take this to mean that it is not serious. Further deterioration can often be prevented simply by stopping any further heat loss (see page 136). Beyond this stage, however, the problems become far worse. We now enter a phase which can be called *moderate hypothermia*, in which the victim may refuse to acknowledge that there is anything wrong. He may become abusive, even violent, and as the body tries harder to prevent further heat loss, the process of vaso-constriction will continue to the point where even shivering will cease. Indeed, because of the reduced blood supply, all muscular movement will be sluggish, and it will take a long time for the body to recover after increasingly frequent falls. At about 33°C, the drop in core temperature will start to affect the vital organs, the most notice-able effects being on the brain and vision. Irrational behaviour (e.g. taking off clothes), incoherence, hallucinations and other forms of visual disturbance are common, and amnesia can occur.

Make no mistake about it: people suffering from moderate hypothermia are very ill. Damage to the vital organs will be such that the prevention of further heat loss will be insufficient to promote recovery, and the victim will have to be actively re-warmed.

When the core temperature falls to below about 31°C, the victim enters the *severely hypothermic* phase, a critical condition in which both pulse and respiration will start to weaken, and the pupils may start to dilate. Below about 30°C, the heartbeat will become shallow and irregular, and the victim will drift towards a coma. Even if the heat loss is stopped immediately, death will result within a matter of a few hours unless medical help is on hand. Indeed, a number of chemical changes will have taken place within the body which can cause fatal complications on rewarm-ing, so it is imperative that anyone who is severely hypothermic gets expert medical help as a matter of extreme urgency.

Below 29°C lies the *acutely hypothermic* phase in which most reflexes cease to function. Below 28°C the vital functions will begin to fail. It is, however, imperative that you do not take the absence of breathing or pulse to indicate death; the low core temperature means that only a small amount of oxygen is required by the body, and there have been cases where apparently dead victims have made full recoveries.

It is, of course, of little use knowing these signs and symptoms if you do not know what to do. Again, it will be helpful to look at each phase in turn.

The most common mistake after having diagnosed the onset of the condition, particularly in a remote situation, is to head urgently towards the nearest habitation. This can be totally the wrong thing to do (unless it is very close by) for any additional expenditure of energy by the victim may cause his core temperature to plummet, possibly with fatal results. No matter where you are, the most important thing to do is to stop any further heat loss, and the best way to do this is to find some form of shelter from the wind. You may even have to construct this yourself.

Once in shelter, replace the victim's wet clothes with dry, spare clothing, and put him into a survival bag which has been insulated from the ground with a sleepmat, rucksacks, clothing – anything. You should now try actively to rewarm him, the best way being for someone to lie in the survival bag with him. If you can give him hot drinks and some high-energy food (your emergency rations), so much the better, A sleeping bag will also be useful, but make sure that someone else has warmed it first—the victim's skin temperature may be so low that he is unable to warm a cold sleeping bag himself.

Although it is important to stop heat loss and to start some form of rewarming, it is important that you do this generally and not locally. This is where a basic understanding of the body's heat-control mechanisms is important. If you warm the body locally, as would happen, for example, in massage, vigorous rubbing, or intense local heating, you could reverse the effects of vaso-constriction. This would lead to the capillaries opening, and warm core blood would be replaced by cold shell blood, with serious consequences. Giving alcohol to a hypothermic person would have the same effect, for one of the effects of alcohol is to dilate the capillaries.

Do not forget, also, that psychology plays an important part in the treatment of any ailment: calm reassurance can literally make the difference between life and death. And think, too, of yourself and of the rest of the party. If conditions are such that one person is hypothermic, the chances are that others may be at risk, and this will be increased if they are hanging around, doing nothing.

Recovery from the mild hypothermic phase can be rapid. However, the victim will have been severely weakened by the experience, and even if he appears to have recovered totally, you should not attempt to carry on with the walk. If you are satisfied that recovery has been made, lead him gently back to the nearest civilisation along the easiest route.

If conditions worsen, or if recovery has not occurred within two hours, you should suspect that the victim has entered the moderately hypothermic phase in which any further heat loss could soon prove fatal. Although the treatment continues to be the same, there are certain other considerations. If, on diagnosis, you suspect the victim already to have reached this phase, you will have to think very carefully before removing his wet clothing for this will contain a certain amount of heat, albeit minimal. Removing this clothing may therefore result in a heat loss, and this must be avoided at all costs. It would be better, therefore, to place the victim, wet clothes and all, into a survival bag, adding extra insulation over the top of the wet clothes.

Even when the heat loss is stopped, recovery from the moderate hypothermic phase will not occur without the application of some form of external heat. Although this is often done by having a fit person lie beside the victim, the rewarming effect can be minimal. If the victim is conscious, you can feed him hot, sweet drinks, either from a flask or freshly made. If the group is carrying a tent, it may be possible to pitch this and carry the victim inside, as many members of the party as possible staying in the tent with him in order to try and raise the temperature.

Sufferers from moderate hypothermia should always be regarded as stretcher cases, even if they appear to have made a total recovery. Self-help is extremely difficult in such situations, and you would be well advised to summon some form of help at the earliest opportunity.

If the victim reaches the severe or acutely hypothermic phase, the situation becomes extremely grave indeed. No matter what action is taken to reverse the heat loss, death will result in a matter of a few hours unless specialist medical assistance is available. All that can be done in the field is to prevent further heat loss, and to provide general (*not local*) rewarming.

Three final points are worth reiterating. Firstly, assuming that you know the victim reasonably well, any uncharacteristic behaviour in poor conditions should be thought of as being indicative of exhaustion-exposure. Your normally mild-mannered companion may, for example, start to swear and become aggressive.

Secondly, you are in a far better position to judge the condition of the victim than is the victim himself. Indeed, he may well deny that there is any problem. Despite these denials, it is important that treatment begins as soon as possible. Prompt action is the key to successful treatment and recovery.

Finally, exhaustion-exposure is avoidable. If you wear the correct clothing and are not over-ambitious, it should never be a problem.

Other ailments

Blisters

Blisters are one of the most common complaints suffered by walkers and anyone who has suffered from even a mild blister when on a long walk will know how painful they can be. However, like exhaustion-exposure, blisters are avoidable.

A blister is simply the result of friction, this friction being caused most commonly by one of four main reasons: badly fitting boots, badly fitting socks, sensitive feet or foreign bodies. Additionally, even if you have bought the correct pair of boots, they may cause blisters simply because they are incorrectly laced, or even because you are not used to walking in them. A good boot, whether of modern or traditional design, needs time to adjust, to mould itself to the shape of your foot. New boots, therefore, are far more likely to give you blisters than boots you have worn on countless walks.

In order to reduce the likelihood of blisters, you can do several things. Firstly, you will obviously need a pair of well fitting boots, as discussed in Chapter 4. Secondly, your socks, too, need to fit you correctly. If they are too small, they will cramp the foot, possibly resulting in blisters along the tops of the toes; if they are too big, there will be folds of material which will affect the fit of the boot. Additionally, it is a false economy to darn walking socks because, however good the repair, there is always a slight 'lump', and this is almost guaranteed to give you blisters.

Thirdly, before putting on the boot, make sure that there is nothing in it (or on your sock) which might cause a blister. Even the smallest piece of grit can cause potential problems. If there is an irremovable lump in the boot (such as could be caused, on a more traditional boot, by a protruding nail or screw), you should have it attended to professionally.

Finally, when you put on your boots, make sure that the tongues are located correctly and that they are laced evenly. Any uncomfortable fold of leather or uneven pressure may get worse as time goes on.

Even if you take all these precautions, you may still run the risk of blisters simply because you are hammering your feet. However, a full blister can be avoided easily by prompt action. Immediately you feel a 'hot spot' – a sore area which marks the site of a potential blister – stop, remove the boot, make sure that there is nothing in the boot or the sock which is causing the problem, then pad the affected area with moleskin, a fabric plaster or a blister pad, all of which can be obtained from most good outdoor equipment shops and also from many chemists. Although it is sometimes inconvenient to stop immediately a hot spot is felt, it is far better to do this than to continue until a blister has formed. If, however, you do get a blister, the best treatment is to burst it gently with a pin which you must sterilise by holding it in a flame until it glows red hot. Gently press the blister to remove all the fluid but on no account remove the skin. Once the fluid has gone, cover the affected area with a sterile dressing held in place with moleskin or a fabric plaster. Alternatively, you can use some of the amazingly effective artificial skin which is becoming more widely available. On toes, the best form of protection is artificial skin held in place with micropore bandage.

One point worth noting is that, if the blister is large, you must be careful to cut both the padding and the material with which it is held in place in such a way that it does not crease, for the underlying skin will be very sensitive, and any unevenness could easily form yet another blister.

Once you arrive home (or at your campsite), remove the boots, socks and any dressing, wash your feet to reduce the chance of infection and let the blister breathe. If you want to walk again within the next few days, cover the affected area with artificial skin before you set out, and make sure that your feet are kept clean.

Heat stroke

Heat stroke is caused by a rise in core temperature and, although less frequent in the British climate than exhaustion-exposure, can be just as serious.

In hot weather, particularly in humid conditions, the heat gained through the muscular activity of walking may be so intense that the body is unable to maintain a heat balance. As overheating begins to occur, the capillaries will dilate and the production of sweat will increase dramatically. Even if this mechanism increases cooling to a sufficient degree, the loss of the fluid and salt contained in sweat can result in several problems, most noticeably that of heat cramp, the first stage of heat stroke.

Heat cramp usually affects the muscles of the legs and abdomen, and is extremely painful. Additionally, the capillaries may have dilated to such an extent that the blood flow to the brain is reduced, leading to faintness. Treatment should be immediate. What is required is some form of shade, and if there is no natural shade, you will have to construct your own. The victim should be allowed to rest in as cool a position as possible, his cramp can be eased by stretching and massaging the affected muscle, and he should be given plenty of water to drink. The addition of a little salt at the rate of a couple of pinches per litre (but no more) will help, as will some form of fruit-flavoured electrolyte replacement drink.

Prompt action will almost invariably result in rapid recovery but, as with hypothermia, there should be no question of continuing the journey as the victim will have been severely weakened. You should head slowly for home along the easiest and coolest route.

The next stage is known as *heat exhaustion*. In this, the core temperature has risen and sweating has continued to such a marked extent that there is a danger of dehydration. The victim will complain of nausea and headache, will be fatigued and light-headed, and may vomit or faint. Both pulse and respiration rates may increase as more and more blood is passed to the extremities, and his skin will, paradoxically, feel cold and clammy.

Again, shade is of the utmost importance, but liquid should only be given in sips because the victim may not be able to keep it down. What you must do is try to increase the amount of heat loss, and this can often be done by loosening clothing, fanning or applying damp clothes to the forehead and the skin. Although it will take far longer for a person to recover from this stage of heat stroke, recovery will usually occur given time, but it is important that the victim be given plenty of time to rest in cool conditions before being led gently homewards. Not only can heat exhaustion recur with frightening ease, but it is also only a small step away from the final stage of *heat stroke*, which is a critical condition.

In this final stage, the core temperature will have increased to such a level that the body functions begin to deteriorate. One of the first things to malfunction will be the ability to dilate and constrict the capillaries, and this will result in a condition in which the body becomes unable to lose heat. As a result, the core temperature will rise rapidly, and the victim will die within a very short period.

Because heat-stroke victims will be suffering from a breakdown of the vital functions, they may display many of the signs and symptoms of exhaustion-exposure, particularly those of irrational behaviour, aggression and abuse. In addition, the skin will either be red, hot and dry or – somewhat confusingly – cool, pale and damp. The temperature of the core could well be as high as 41°C by this stage, and immediate and active cooling is imperative. It will not be sufficient simply to put the victim in shade. Remove clothing, fan him vigorously, and – if possible – place damp clothes or cool water against the forehead or the back of the neck. Only give liquid if he is conscious, and then only in sips.

Victims of heat stroke are critically ill and should be regarded as stretcher cases. Medical advice should be sought in all cases, even if they appear to make a complete recovery.

As with exhaustion-exposure, the condition is avoidable. On particularly hot days, avoid strenuous walking wherever possible and drink plenty of liquid. If you eat a balanced diet it should be unnecessary for you to have salt tablets, but some people may find them useful. If you decide to use salt tablets, they should be taken in the morning as a precautionary measure and not used as an item of first-aid after the event.

Frost-nip

At the other extreme, frost-nip is a condition to which those who enjoy walking in particularly cold conditions are susceptible. It is caused mainly by acute vaso-constriction, in which the warm blood supply to the extremities is reduced to such a degree that the cells actually begin to freeze. However, wearing tight clothing which restricts the blood supply will have a similar effect, so it is important that articles of clothing such as gloves and mittens, socks and boots fit well. The areas most commonly affected are the toes and fingers, the ears, nose and cheeks.

If you are walking in particularly cold conditions and any of the above areas begin to feel warm or numb after having been cold or painful, you should suspect frost-nip. If you inspect the area, it will probably have the appearance and feel of white candle wax. The treatment is both simple and effective: rewarming. On no account, however, should you rub the affected area, for you are likely to damage the frozen cells. Recovery is usually rapid, but may be accompanied by pins-and-needles, stinging and often pain. It is also worth bearing in mind that once an area has suffered from frost-nip, it will be permanently weakened and is far more likely to be affected in the future. Prevention is far better than cure, and is easy if you wear the correct clothing.

If the freezing is allowed to continue, the inevitable result will be superficial frostbite in which the cells begin to rupture and die. Although treatment is essentially the same, it is even more imperative that no massaging or rubbing takes place. Recovery is not so easy, and you should seek medical advice at the earliest possible opportunity. If you intend to undertake mountain walking in winter conditions you would be wise to read more about the subject.

Although superficial frostbite should not pose a threat to a fit or well clothed person, it is an ever-present danger to victims of accidents (particularly where bones have been broken) or victims of exhaustion-exposure, and you should bear this in mind when treating such casualties in cold conditions.

Other ailments

When walking in snow, there is a danger of **snow blindness**, an excruciatingly painful condition caused by ultra-violet light reflecting from the surface of the snow. If you walk in such conditions, you should wear good sunglasses with ultra-violet screening lenses.

Similarly, **sun-burn** can potentially be very serious, and no matter how much of a sun worshipper you may be, you should always carry (and regularly apply) a good sun-screen whilst you are out.

Finally, if you have to take a regular medication, such as would be the case in diabetes, for example, not only should you take a more than sufficient supply of medication with you, but you should also carry some form of card which tells people what and how much you take, and why. This information will obviously be essential if you have an accident, particularly if you are unconscious.

Conclusion

General safety is very much an attitude of mind which has as its central core a deep respect for the environment in which you walk, whether this be along country lanes or amongst the crags of

29. *Descending to Pen y Pass in central Snowdonia – the end of a perfect walking day*

remote mountains. This environment will never be actively hostile, but it will always be insensitive to any form of human suffering. Your surroundings will never help you if you get into difficulties, but you may be able to use them. The only way that you will be able to do this is through experience.

Assuming that you are correctly clothed and shod for the type of walking you enjoy, have the minimal amount of essential equipment, understand the principles behind a few of the techniques which will help you through difficult terrain, know how to use your map and compass and are sensible when it comes to taking risks, you will not go far wrong.

I chose to divide this book into a number of sections in the hope that such division may make it easier to use as a source of reference. Your walking will rarely be divided in such a way. It is the way in which you combine all these these snippets of information which can make walking comfortable or uncomfortable, which can make your situation safe or insecure, which can cause you to enjoy the experience or swear, 'never again'.

Appendix I
The Country
Code

Guard against all risk of fire...
Heaths, plantations, woodlands and fellsides are all highly inflammable and even sparks can be dangerous. If you do build a fire, always have someone watching it, and make sure it is completely extinguished before departure. If you discover a fire, try to stamp it out. If you cannot, report it immediately to the Fire Brigade, Police, or Forestry Commission Officers.

Leave all gates as you find them...
Gates on public rights of way should be unlocked. If not, there should be a stile nearby. Where there is no stile and the gates are unlocked, open and close them as opposed to climbing over them. If already open, leave them open.

Keep dogs under proper control...
Generally speaking, you should keep your dog on a lead whenever there is livestock around, and when you are walking along narrow country roads.

Keep to paths across farmland...
Follow footpaths carefully. If travelling from valley areas to the open fells, make sure you find the correct paths.

Avoid damaging fences, hedges and walls...
Always use the gates and stiles provided, even if the path detours to reach them. You should not have to cross a wall, fence or hedge by any other means than a stile or gate if you are on a public footpath.

If there is no gate or stile, detour until you reach a point where you can cross with ease and without risk of causing damage.

Leave no litter...
Take *all* your litter home with you. There is no excuse for leaving anything behind. Leave the countryside as you would wish to find it. Do

not bury litter; animals may dig it up again, and remember that opened tins, plastic bags and broken glass can be fatal to both domestic and wild animals.

Safeguard water supplies...
Many farms and isolated rural communities rely directly on springs as their sole source of drinking water. Do not build dams or pollute these springs in any way, nor pollute cattle troughs or any other form of water storage or water supply.

Protect wildlife, wild plants and tress...
The countryside is best seen, not collected. Do not pick wild flowers, disturb wild animals or birds, carve your initials on trees or leave graffiti of any description. Apart from other considerations, you may well be committing an offence if you do.

Go carefully on country roads...
Country roads are often narrow and winding, with high banks or hedges. When travelling by vehicle, drive slowly and carefully, and be considerate to other road users. Slow to a crawl if you meet people on horseback and, if the road is narrow, stop and let the horses pass you. Neither rev the engine nor sound the horn.

When walking along such roads, place yourself in the position of greatest visibility and listen for oncoming traffic. You will often hear a vehicle long before the driver can see you.

Respect the life of the countryside...
Many people live and work in the country. Respect not only their property, but also their livelihood and privacy. Always obtain the permission of the landowner before pitching a tent.

Appendix II
The Mountain
Code

Be prepared ...
Make sure you are correctly clothed and equipped for the proposed walk and the possible weather conditions.

Always carry waterproofs, spare sweater, map and compass, whistle, first-aid kit, emergency food and a polythene survival bag. In winter you should take extra spare clothing and emergency food, and a good torch.

Never undertake a walk or expedition which is beyond your training, experience, or fitness.

Do not go into the mountains alone unless you are very experienced.

Check the *local* weather forecast before you set off on your walk, and do not be afraid to alter your plans if the conditions are, or are likely to become, inclement.

Disused mines and quarries in mountainous areas rarely have any safety checks. Keep away from such sites.

Never venture onto snow and ice until you are thoroughly familiar with basic winter techniques and conditions. Mastering the use of an ice axe and crampons should be regarded as a *minimum* level of ability.

In the event of an accident, carry out immediate first aid and get the casualty off the hill. If you cannot do this yourself, erect a shelter for the casualty and the rest of the group and use the International Mountain Distress Signal (see below). Other people may be nearby and in a position to help. If evacuation is impossible, find a telephone, dial 999 and ask for the Police, then ask for Mountain Rescue.

The International Mountain Distress Signal is six rapid signals (by whistle, torch, shouting, etc.) repeated at intervals of one minute. This should be repeated until you are located. The answer is three rapid signals repeated at intervals of one minute.

Respect the land...

Keep to public rights of way and permitted footpaths, especially when travelling in enclosed areas and across land where special access agreements have been made.

Avoid crossing firing ranges and game shooting areas. When north of the border, remember the Scottish Deer Stalking Season (August/September).

If you do not wish to camp on an official campsite, make sure you have the permission of the landowner before you pitch your tent.

Take *all* your litter home. If you bury it, animals may dig it up. Empty tins and plastic bags are particularly dangerous to wildlife. Glass bottles are totally unnecessary.

Conserve wildlife...

Do your utmost to disturb neither domestic nor wild animals, and leave flowers and plants for everyone to enjoy.

Do not pollute mountain streams by dam-building, dish-washing, or any other activity. Any form of pollution can seriously affect the ecology of such streams and their surroundings.

Take nothing but photographs;
Leave nothing but goodwill;
Disturb nothing but the air around you.

Consider other people...

Never throw stones or any other objects over the tops of crags or down slopes, even if you cannot see anyone below you. There may well be climbers or other walkers hidden from view. If you accidentally dislodge a stone, immediately warn anyone who may be below you, shouting the standard call 'Below!'.

Many mountaineers leave tents and rucksacks whilst they go off on a rock climb. Do not remove apparently deserted equipment.

Many people live and work in the mountains. Have consideration for their way of life and their privacy.

Only lead walks and expeditions when you are competent to do so.

Most people go into the mountains to enjoy the peace and quiet of their surroundings. Do nothing that would spoil their enjoyment.

Be weatherwise...

Even in summer, weather conditions can change with incredible speed. Do not hesitate to turn back if the weather deteriorates; only fools press on regardless.

Low cloud or mist will substantially reduce the speed of most parties. Be careful in such conditions. Walk at a speed which allows you to see as much as possible of the ground ahead.

After heavy rain, the crossing of many mountain streams may be impossible. Rather than attempting unorthodox crossing methods, detour until you find a safe crossing point.

Both summer and winter weather extremes pose particular problems for mountain walkers. You should know both the symptoms and treatment of heat exhaustion and hypothermia (exhaustion-exposure).

Walking expeditions in high, craggy mountain areas may require specialist skills, including the use of ropes. Winter mountain walking, especially in Scotland, can be a most serious undertaking. Apart from the hazards posed by cornices and avalanche-prone slopes, daylight hours are far less and general conditions are usually far more extreme than elsewhere in Britain.

(Based upon *The Mountain Code*, published by the British Mountaineering Council)

Appendix III
Useful
Organisations

Walking is becoming such a popular pastime that you are almost certain to find a club of some description in your area. Details can usually be found in the back of the relevant magazines, or you can write to one of the major bodies, such as:

THE RAMBLERS' ASSOCIATION
1–5 Wandsworth Road, London SW8 2LJ   Tel. 01-582-6826.

THE BACKPACKERS' CLUB
20 St Michael's Road, Tilehurst, Reading RG3 4RP.

THE LONG-DISTANCE WALKERS' ASSOCIATION
7 Ford Drive, Yarnfield, Stone, Staffordshire ST15 0RP.

If you are interested in mountain walking, you might like to contact:

BRITISH MOUNTAINEERING COUNCIL
Crawford House, Precinct Centre, Booth Street Est, Manchester M13 9RZ. Tel. 061-273-5835 (general enquiries & membership)
061-273-5839 (publications, courses, etc.)
061-273-5163 (insurance, reciprocal rights card).

Details of Scottish clubs can be obtained from the secretary of the Mountaineering Council of Scotland, address obtainable from:

SCOTTISH SPORTS COUNCIL
1 St Colme Street, Edinburgh EH3 6AA.   Tel. 031-225-8411.

Courses in various aspects of walking and mountaincraft are run at the Sports Council's National Centres:

PLAS-Y-BRENIN
Capel Curig, Nr Betws-y-Coed, Gwynedd LL24 0ET
Tel. 06904-280 (bookings)
06904-214 or 363 (offices).

PLAS-MENAI
Llanfairisgaer, Caernarfon, Gwynedd   Tel. 0248-670964.

GLENMORE LODGE
Aviemore, Inverness-shire PH22 1QU   Tel. 047-986-276 (bookings)
047-986-256 (offices).

In addition, there are many other excellent organisations which offer holidays and courses to individuals and groups. Their addresses can be found in relevant magazines. The author offers courses in various aspects of walking and mountaincraft, full details of which are available from:

KEVIN WALKER MOUNTAIN ACTIVITIES
James Street, Llangynidr, Crickhowell, Powys NP8 1NN
Tel. 0874-730554.

Information on the National Parks can be obtained from the Information Officer at the relevant address:

BRECON BEACONS NATIONAL PARK
7 Glamorgan Street, Brecon, Powys LD3 7DP   Tel. 0874-4437.

DARTMOOR NATIONAL PARK
Parke, Haytor Road, Bovey Tracey, Newton Abbott, Devon TQ13 9JQ   Tel. 0626-832093.

EXMOOR NATIONAL PARK
Exmoor House, Dulverton, Somerset   Tel. 0398-23665.

LAKE DISTRICT NATIONAL PARK
Brockhole, Windermere, Cumbria LA23 1LJ   Tel. 09662-3467.

NORTHUMBERLAND NATIONAL PARK
Eastburn, South Park, Hexham, Northumberland NE46 1BS
Tel. 0434-605555.

NORTH YORK MOORS NATIONAL PARK
The Old Vicarage, Bondgate, Helmsley, North Yorkshire YO6 5BP
Tel. 04392-657.

PEAK DISTRICT NATIONAL PARK
Losehill Hall, Castleton, Derbyshire S30 2WB   Tel. 0433-20373.

PEMBROKESHIRE COAST NATIONAL PARK
County Offices, Haverfordwest, Dyfed SA61 1QZ   Tel. 0437-4591

SNOWDONIA NATIONAL PARK
Penrhyndeudraeth, Gwynedd LL48 6LS   Tel. 0766-770274.

YORKSHIRE DALES NATIONAL PARK
Colvend, Hebden Road, Grassington, Skipton, North Yorkshire BD23 5LB   Tel. 0756-752748.

Information about walking in Scotland can be obtained from:

THE SCOTTISH RIGHTS OF WAY SOCIETY
6 Abercromby Place, Edinburgh

For Details of the official long-distance footpaths (National Trails):

THE COUNTRYSIDE COMMISSION
John Dower House, Crescent Place, Cheltenham, Gloucestershire GL50 3RA   Tel. 0242-21381.

Appendix IV
Further Reading

There is a wealth of literature about walking, as a visit to any bookshop or library will show. There is so much good material available that it is not easy to know what to advise people to read. Although the following list is far from comprehensive and has a definite 'upland' bias, I have tried to give a fair coverage of the subjects, and you are almost certain to find something of interest.

Although some of the books listed are now out of print, they may still be available from second hand book shops or public libraries.

Information and Instruction

Avalanche and Snow Safety, Colin Fraser, Murray, London, 1978.

Backpackers Manual, The, Cameron McNeish, Oxford Illustrated Press, Yeovil, 1984.

First Aid for Hillwalkers, Jane Renouf and Stewart Hulse, Cicerone, Cumbria, 1982.

Footpaths of Britain, The, Michael Marriot, Macdonald Futura, London, 1981.

Let's Walk, Mark Linley, Meridian Books, Wharley, 1988.

Mountaincraft and Leadership, Eric Langmuir, Scottish Sports Council/ MLTB, Edinburgh, 1984.

Mountaineering (The Freedom of the Hills), ed. Peters, The Mountaineers, Seattle, 1982.

Mountaineering First Aid, Lentz, Macdonald, and Carline, The Mountaineers, Seattle, 1985.

Mountain Hazards, Kevin Walker, Constable, London, 1988.

Mountain Navigation Techniques, Kevin Walker, Constable, London, 1986.

Mountain Weather for Climbers, David Unwin, Cordee, Leicester, 1978.

Safety on Mountains, British Mountaineering Council, Manchester, 1975.

Start Backpacking, Mike Marriott, Stanley Paul, London, 1981.

Wild Country Camping, Kevin Walker, Constable, London, 1989.

General Interest

Classic Walks, Ken Wilson and Richard Gilbert, Diadem, London, 1982.
High Adventure, Edmund Hillary, Hodder & Stoughton, London, 1955.
Mountaineering in Scotland/Undiscovered Scotland, W. H. Murray, Diadem, London, 1979.
Next Horizon, Chris Bonington, Hodder & Stoughton, London, 1976.
Nothing Venture, Nothing Win, Edmund Hillary, Hodder & Stoughton, London, 1975.
The Games Climbers Play, ed. Ken Wilson, Diadem, London, 1978.
The Shining Mountain, Peter Boardman, Hodder & Stoughton, London, 1987.
The Winding Trail, ed. Roger Smith, Diadem, London, 1981.
Wild Walks, Richard Gilbert & Ken Wilson, Diadem, London, 1988.

Magazines

The Great Outdoors, Climber & Hillwalker, Footloose, High (journal of the British Mountaineering Council), *Outdoor Action, Pursuit, Wilderness Odyssey, Rambler* (journal of the Rambler's Association), etc.

Many of the above carry stories, articles and gear tests, as well as items of news and gossip. There are also directories of equipment retailers and clubs, and the magazines are excellent sources of information.

Index